I'm a Fixer-Upper

A Day-by-Day Remodeling Guide

Audrey
Fix your eyes on Jesus
Heb 12:2.
Alene

Alene Snodgrass

A Contemporary Bible Study for Today's Woman
A Six Week Study for Individual and Group Use

PRESS

www.xulonpress.com

Contents

Acknowledgements

I want to thank my hubby, Curt, for being my number one cheerleader. Without his constant, encouraging words nudging me to write, I'd still be sitting at the computer.

There are many girlfriends I need to thank for keeping me accountable to finishing what the Lord had put on my heart to study and write. Thank you also to my online buddies. You totally rock!

And, of course, a huge round of applause goes to the *I'm a Fixer-Upper* Bible study pilot group. These women spent endless hours studying, editing, and critiquing this study. God moved in magnificent ways through our time together.

Thanks specifically to:

Debra Scott-Brown
Esmie Fisher
Laura Howard
Laura Harris
Pat Larsen
Carol Pearson
Brenda Revett
Sandra Staley
Holly Thompson

Thank you to Jennifer Hanchey. Your editing expertise is greatly appreciated.

As I thank my God for being the Master Renovator and being ever so patient with me, I also thank Him for each of you.

Thank you, Lord, for taking our run down grass huts and restoring them to gorgeous palaces.

About This Book

$\mathcal{C}$an you relate to feeling like a fixer-upper? I know I can. 1 Peter 2:5 says, "You also, like living stones, are being built into a spiritual house." In other words, you and I are God's house. That thought alone is so magnificent it's hard to comprehend. It's no wonder I feel like a renovation project.

Welcome to the study *I'm a Fixer-Upper.* You will join me in a day by day remodeling process for your spiritual house. This Bible study book is organized in six weekly lessons. Each week's lesson is broken into five daily studies that you can complete in about thirty minutes. If you would like to spend more time studying, there are ample scriptures for additional reflection. In addition to this book, you will need a Bible, a spiral notebook or journal, and a pen or pencil for this study. You will use the spiral notebook or journal to record your thoughts, ideas, and answers to the questions provided.

In each lesson there are scriptures that emphasize your day's lesson. I encourage you to look them up and write them in your spiral or make notes in your own Bible for future reference. Taking the time to look them up and write them out will help you remember more vividly what they mean, how they spoke to you, and where they are found.

This is an interactive study that provides opportunities for your expression and response.

- Reflection times are marked by an indented paragraph like this. Please do not skip these exercises as they as crucial to the development of the study and the renovation of God's house.

To get the most out of this study, you are encouraged to think about or act upon **Today's Remodeling Tip.** These quick tips, ideas, and activities keep you focused on your day to day remodeling plan for your spiritual house and your life.

For Leaders: *I'm a Fixer-Upper* is a study for individual or small group use. There is great benefit in working through this study with other women. No matter where you are in your walk, you will find the insights and encouragement of others helpful along this journey. Your small group should meet once a week for discussion. This study is perfect for a seven-week Bible study. Spend the first week on the introduction, discussing the theme verse and getting to know your group. Thereafter, the format for an hour Bible study might be ten minutes for gathering and opening prayer and forty minutes for discussion, using the reflection questions. The last ten minutes would be well spent on prayer requests and group prayer.

Before you begin, please commit your study to the Lord. Ask the Lord to guide you and give you a passion for His house where renovation, restoration, and renewal will take place.

Girls, grab your hard hats. It's time to get serious about reno-vating your life because "[you] can do everything through him who gives [you] strength" (Phil. 4:13). Whether you are a construction worker or a girly-girl, this study is for you.

Introduction

*W*hen was the last time you remodeled or renovated your residence? Do you walk through your home constantly noticing the well-worn and stained carpet, marks on the walls, and old beat up furniture? The flaws you notice may depress you. You are home; however, you feel disconnected and dissatisfied. Something isn't right.

Can you relate? As I wrote this study, we were under construction in the remodeling of our home. I'm tired of dust, grit, and tools! Sometimes I have that same attitude about renovating and remodeling my spiritual life. I continually feel like a fixer-upper. Oh, I've tried spiritual makeovers and overhauls. I can easily testify that I'd much rather have a beauty makeover than get down and dirty to deal with my real issues: prayerlessness, lack of forgiveness, bitterness, anger, or lack of self control. I know what needs to be renovated and restored inside, but it's easy to get by (or fool others) with cleaning up my language, applying a coat of make-up, and overhauling my wardrobe.

To set the record straight, I'm not your steel-toed boot kind of girl. I am not in love with the rigors of demolition and construction. However, I am a real woman living a real life. I guarantee you I don't have a housekeeper that spruces up my house (though I confess I would love one). I do the chores, tend to my family, and follow, as best as I can, God's action plan. I am willing to do hard work for my house.

In the weeks ahead, you'll begin fixing up your spiritual home by applying Biblical truths. You will read about the first house plans God ordered for the tabernacle so He could come and live among His people. Throughout this study, you will focus on God's temple. If you are a believer, *you* are God's house: "We are God's house, if we keep our courage and remain confident in our hope in Christ" (Heb. 3:6 NLT).

From today forward, you'll repair, restore, and renovate God's house using His Word as your blueprint. You will walk away from this study refurbished and refreshed, knowing that your foundation is secure and the rooms of your soul are swept clean. Push up your sleeves, put on your hardhat, and pull on your gloves—remodeling is about to begin.

Week One

Tents, Tabernacles, and Temples—Oh, My

re you a history buff? I'm not. Seriously, I could care less. History never interested me in high school or college. As a matter of fact, (Mom, you might want to skip this sentence.) I think I cheated my way through all those classes. Shortly after college, I married a military man, and we lived in Germany. We visited many cities, castles, and even a concentration camp. My husband, Curt, couldn't understand how I could be so clueless. He'd often ask things like, "Don't you remember this city from your history lessons? Remember the story of King Ludwig II? Alene, can't you recall anything?" Nope, can't say I do!

Because I was never interested in history, I didn't pay much attention to the Old Testament and how things came to be. I tried; I promise. But all I could see was numbers, names, and foreign countries that didn't interest me. Whether you loved history or hated it, I am going to challenge you this week to soak in the history we're going to discover. It will change your life. It has changed mine.

As I dug in to understand the history of God's house, I was blown away with what I discovered. Since day one in the Garden of Eden, all God has wanted to do is to dwell among His people. I think He must be a sanguine personality like me—we love people. Through these abbreviated history lessons this week, I hope you see just how much God loves you.

My prayer for you as we study the history of the tabernacle is that you will come to realize the magnificence and presence of the God who wants to dwell with you.

Day One

Heavenly Dwellings

*D*rive around town in any major city of America, and you'll see street after street of cookie-cutter homes. You'll notice some landscaping changes, but from the floor plans to the front doors, things look pretty much the same.[1] In this book, though, we are going to look at the home located inside of you—God's residence. You'll quickly notice we are all different and your renovation job will be different from mine. To set the scene, we should do a little research and excavation. Let's venture back and take a look at the first heavenly dwelling and see how God's house came to be.

Speaking of venturing back, do you ever wish you could go back in time to see what life was really like in Biblical times? As I was preparing this study, I began studying the tabernacle and temple, and I have to say there were a few times I found myself longing to be there in the temple courtyard.

I'm your everyday girly-girl, so I really didn't want to be there walking among the people, hauling water and bathing in a river. No, I just wanted to "pop in" like Samantha on *Bewitched* for a bird's eye view. With a twitch of my nose, I could find myself sitting atop the city walls, watching Biblical life happen. I wanted to hear the sounds, smell the aroma, and feel the city's heartbeat.

- Take a moment and "pop in" for a bird's eye view of Biblical life. Describe in great detail what you see, hear, and smell. How does it differ from your images of suburban America?

As I have taken this journey to understand what it means to be "built into a spiritual house," I've spent time in thought and prayer and tried to picture myself within the temple (1 Pet. 2:5). There were days I didn't want to leave those thoughts and tend to real life. Those were precious moments when God's holy place came to life within my soul.

In those instances, I began to understand that when God created man in the Garden of Eden, He truly wanted to dwell with Adam and Eve and have a personal relationship. They communed daily until that darned old snake came along. Adam and Eve disobeyed. They decided to run and hide, and they hoped that God wouldn't find out. They tried to avoid the relationship God intended them to have with Him. However, God was still longing to communicate and dwell with them. He ran after them calling out, "Where are you?" God pursued them. He longed to live with them, not in a superficial neighborhood, but in the beautiful Garden of Eden.

Just like Adam and Eve, I've been guilty of running away from God. Becoming aware of my sin, escape seemed like the logical thing to do—RUN! Yet, God continued to cry out, "Where are you?" (Gen. 3: 8, 9).

- Are you trying to run from being God's heavenly dwelling? Do you hear Him calling out to you? If so, what is He saying?

God longs to be with you. Not only does He want to be with you, but you should also long to be close to Him. You can't hide out in your neighborhood forever. Sooner or later, your heart will burn with desire to know the true and living God.

- Write out 1 Corinthians 3:16, 17 in modern day language. What does this verse say to you specifically?

You are God's temple. God's Spirit lives in you. But it gets even better: while you are tending to your spiritual house and God's dwelling place, Jesus is making plans and arrangements for your eternal home. You've got to hear this! Jesus says, "In my Father's house are many rooms; if it were not so, I would have told you. I am going there to prepare a place for you. And if I go and prepare a place for you, I will come back and take you to be with me that you also may be where I am" (John 14:2, 3).

- Describe what Jesus is preparing. Is it a mansion? Is it more like a hotel? Maybe a cookie-cutter neighborhood? How would you want your heavenly home to look? Do you wonder if there will even be a building?

Oh my goodness, my house and yours will be the most glorious houses ever with the coolest address, no matter if it's a building or a cumulus cloud. Girl, I hope my home is next door to yours!

King David must have understood how God longs to dwell with His people as he penned, "One thing I ask of the LORD, this is what I seek: that I may dwell in the house of the LORD all the days of my life, to gaze upon the beauty of the LORD and to seek him in his temple" (Ps. 27:4).

Think about something. Not only can you dwell in the house of the Lord all the days of your life, but you can live there forever and ever for all eternity. Take a moment and quiet your mind so you can truly grasp how awesome it is to live with God. God is not only living in heaven, He also dwells within each of us through His Spirit. Even now, He is preparing a place for us. Feel the calm, peace, and serenity of these promises.

Are you ready to avoid the rat race of suburban living? Would you like peace today? Why wait? Join us tomorrow as we study Moses and the first home set up specifically to commune with God. God comes to dwell with his people.

Today's Remodeling Tip:

Put away all your preconceived ideas of where God lives. He doesn't live at the church building. You are His spiritual residence. Write out your new thoughts about God's residence.

Day Two

Mobile Homes

*B*eing the wife of a military officer for twenty-three years has given me the opportunity to experience my fair share of moving. We packed up our home and moved every two to three years to different parts of the world. Hallelujah for moving companies!

I have since helped friends who didn't have the luxury of professional moving companies. What a chore! Packing boxes and sorting through household clutter is not my cup of tea. The work and hassle didn't end there either. There was also the chore of breaking down and loading furniture, kids' toys, and yard equipment. Not to mention having to arrange each piece in the moving truck as if it were a jigsaw puzzle. Where are those full service transport companies when you need them? There was a time, however, when no such company existed. Can you imagine a time before U-Haul®?

Glancing through Genesis, you notice families lived in tents. When it was time to move, they packed up their mobile homes and moved out. It was much different than today's relocations. Except for a few instances, when a move took place, the whole tent city moved. It wasn't one family getting relocated due to a job transfer; instead, the whole camp packed up their tents and headed out.

I'm not sure how you picture that scene, but my mind pictures chaos. We aren't talking about a few men gathering up their tents, throwing their goods on their donkeys, and heading out. They had wives, families, servants, and livestock. Can you imagine moving with kids, kids, and more kids under foot? Plus, traveling with pets is never fun, much less a whole herd of cows and sheep. Imagine the dust, grit, and sand—not to mention the cow patties.

I can easily say there was one thing I liked about moving every few years. I knew that my house and everything in it was going to get a good once over. If there was clutter, it was thrown away. If an item was filthy, it was cleaned. If it was disorganized, it would be organized. If it was dusty, it was polished. I got a fresh start.

I'm positive there were blessings in having to move those tents. At least everything would be swept clean of dust and debris. The grounds where they slaughtered and offered their sacrifices were bound to have been a mess. If you've ever raised or stabled horses, cows, or sheep you can imagine the odor. Plus, their plumbing system wasn't quite as sophisticated as ours. I'm sure they enjoyed the fresh air as they pulled out of the old campsite.

There was one thing I didn't like about moving and that was the feeling of being displaced as I tried to settle into my new city and new home. The hardest thing during the hustle and bustle was staying connected to God. Tranquility and peace were out the door. Through the stressful process of relocating, I'd get overwhelmed with the need to get my life organized. I would get busy and before I knew it, I'd have lost my spiritual peace. I'd begin to feel detached from God.

I'm thinking Moses must have felt that separation as well. There aren't clear records about a church, temple, or tabernacle before God spoke to Moses on Mount Sinai. Even though the people were continually on the move, Moses found a way to be close to God as they moved their tents from town to town:

Now Moses used to take a tent and pitch it outside the camp some distance away, calling it the "tent of meeting." Anyone inquiring of the LORD would go to the tent of meeting outside the camp. And whenever Moses went out to the tent, all the people rose and stood at the entrances to their tents, watching Moses until he entered the tent. As Moses went into the tent, the pillar of cloud would come down and stay at the entrance, while the LORD spoke with Moses. Whenever the people saw the pillar of cloud standing at the entrance to the tent, they all stood and worshiped, each at the entrance to his tent. The LORD would speak to Moses face to face, as a man speaks with his friend. Then Moses would return to the camp (Exod. 33:7-11).

Moses had such a heart for God that he planned and prepared a place to meet with God. This tent of meeting was Moses' special place to get away and have face-to-face communication with God. The Lord knew Moses intimately. This relationship did not happen in the midst of unorganized chaos while moving a tent city or by accident. It happened by Moses setting aside a specific place to meet with God as he traveled through the wilderness. That place was far enough away from the camp that he would be free of distractions. Notice that the whole camp knew when Moses was speaking to God.

- Describe the specific place you meet with the Lord. Can you call this place your tent of meeting where you inquire of the Lord, commune, pray, and linger in His presence? Could you say that all the people in your camp know when you are meeting face to face with God?

God drew Moses to that tent for a relationship. Likewise, many generations later, David heard the Lord calling:

My heart has heard you say, "Come and talk with me."
And my heart responds, "Lord, I am coming."
(Ps. 27:8 NLT)

Whether you live in a travel trailer, mansion, or apartment, God also calls to you. He longs to commune with you. God doesn't just abide in the tent of meeting or the church. He abides in you.

God eventually moves from the mobile home to the tabernacle. Tomorrow you'll see the first blueprint for that spiritual house. But for today, set aside some time and meet with God. He calls out to you, *"Come and talk with me"*. Respond, *"I am coming, Lord!"*

Today's Remodeling Tip:

Drop the excuses for not being able to find a quite place to commune with God. Tomorrow before any "campers" awake at your house, get up and sneak away to your favorite spot and enjoy time with God.

Day Three

The First Blueprints

*T*he first blueprints were nothing like what we'd see at the architect's office today. There were no drawings to follow or duplicate as God laid out His plans. I wonder what Moses thought.

Can you imagine what it was like when God called Moses up to Mount Sinai to reveal His blueprints for the tabernacle, His first home (Exod. 24:15-17)? Once again, I find myself wanting to be there. Imagine Moses entering the cloud where he heard the Lord speak. *Whoa!* My heart aches to speak to God face to face as Moses was accustomed (Exod. 33:11).

As God began speaking to Moses, giving many, many details for the tabernacle, He said, "Tell the Israelites . . ." Now, in my mind, I would be thinking, *Stop, rewind and freeze.* God would have lost me right there. My heart would have been pounding because I can't remember details, much less remember them and then repeat them to others. I would have been scrambling around for a stick to write notes in the sand. Or, without thinking, I'd be blaring out, "God, can you talk a little slower ple-e-e-ease?" Nevertheless, Moses received the lengthy instructions:

The LORD said to Moses, "Tell the Israelites to bring me an offering. You are to receive the offering for me from each man whose heart prompts him to give. These are the offerings you are to receive from them: gold, silver and bronze; blue, purple and scarlet yarn and fine linen; goat hair; ram skins dyed red and hides of sea cows; acacia wood; olive oil for the light; spices for the anointing oil and for the fragrant incense; and onyx stones and other gems to be mounted on the ephod and breastpiece. Then have them make a sanctuary for me, and I will dwell among them. Make this tabernacle and all its furnishing exactly like the pattern I will show you." (Exod. 25:1-9)

God used the word *exactly*. I can feel my blood pressure rising. I don't know how Moses did it *exactly*, but he did. Before we read on to uncover all the meticulous details Moses had to remember, let's look at a couple of things.

I love the authenticity that God requires. He says bring me an offering, but only if your heart prompts you to give. God knows your heart and the last thing He needs is you offering your home and resources with a clinched fist or a stone-cold heart. More than gold, silver, yarn, chandeliers, or money, God wants your heart full of love for Him: "To love him with all your heart, with all your understanding and with all your strength, and to love your neighbor as yourself is more important than all burnt offerings and sacrifices" (Mark 12:33).

To love Him is more important than sacrifice. As you begin to love God wholeheartedly, you'll look forward to bringing Him your ordinary offerings. As you give Him your yarn, oils, spices, and stones, you'll witness God do the extraordinary.

The Israelites brought their offerings as asked, and God began building a tabernacle, a sanctuary. He was furnishing it so that He could dwell among His people.

- Read Exodus 25:10—31:18. Do you think Moses had a hard time remembering all those details? What would have been the hardest thing for you to understand?

Maybe God gave Moses an extra dose of ginkgo biloba for his memory. I'm not sure, but God had a plan to be carried out, and Moses was the man. Reading through all the details, you soon realize how beautiful and significant each one is. God had planned, prepared, and mapped out what His home was to look like long before He gave the details to Moses. From the courtyard, to the lampstand, to the priestly garments, God had the perfect plan for His sanctuary. This is the same planning process that He used in the beginning to create and form the world. Think about all the details and intricacies in your body which He designed and created. Our God is a planning God.

I'm blown away that Moses remembered all those details, but if you are familiar with the story, you know the challenges he faced as he came down off the mountain from being with God for forty days and nights. Thank goodness God helped him with the details by inscribing them on two stone tablets. But who would have known what was to come?

- To refresh your memory, read Exodus 32-33. Why do you think the people began worshiping other gods?

The Israelites proved to be an impatient bunch, a people with wandering hearts: "When the people saw that Moses was so long in coming down from the mountain, they gathered around Aaron and said, 'Come, make us gods who will go before us'" (Exod. 32:1). I want to shout at the Israelites, "Come on, people. Can't you see the consuming fire on the top of the mountain?"

Note that impatience and fear, more often than not, lead to ruin. Throughout Scripture, God calls us to be quiet, to watch and wait, and stay alert: "Be still, and know that I am God" (Ps. 46:10). It is human nature to want evidence that God is moving and working. Instead, God asks us to trust Him. Without trust, there is no faith.

Notice when Aaron and the people were impatient and decided to make idols to worship, they brought goods. They brought their gold earrings. They must have had a lot of earrings! That day, their ordinary offerings did **not** become extraordinary—they became a golden calf. One hunk of gold was turned into another. Mercy, I can hear the girls singing Madonna's *Material Girl* as they danced around the golden idol. Obviously, the people did not have hearts that were sold out to God.

You have to admire Moses, though. He had just spent forty days with God in the most intimate of ways, conversing face to face and getting the blueprints for something so amazing. It was literally a mountaintop experience. He came off the mountain carrying two stone tablets, only to arrive in the midst of total chaos and nonsense. He quickly noticed his family and friends were worshiping a golden calf.

Just as God gave Moses instructions to build His first earthly home (actually it was like a pop-up, fold-down, travel trailer), God has also given you detailed instructions of how to construct and build your spiritual house. His word tells us to be built into spiritual houses (1 Cor. 3:9). As you begin looking into the construction and renovation process, many of your friends and family will not understand. There might be times you grow impatient and want to give up. Keep your eyes on God as you stand at the construction site; don't get impatient or overwhelmed and give up. You are coming from a different camp, so your renovation and remodeling requirements will be different. Don't panic if you don't have all the details yet—God will provide. He is Jehovah Jireh or JJ as Eric Sandras refers to him in *Plastic Jesus*.[2]

- As you wrap up today's lesson, read Exodus 34:1-14. What adjectives would you use to describe God?

God is a God of second chances. He was willing to rewrite the stones or redraw the blueprints for Moses. He was willing to forgive the people who sinned against Him. Yes, the Lord is compassionate and gracious; slow to anger, abounding in love and faithfulness.

You might think your spiritual house is beyond repair, but it's not. He has the perfect blueprint for you. He knows every detail, for He drafted and designed you and is the foundation upon which your house should be built. God has a specific set of plans to dwell among His people. His blueprints are incredible.

Today's Remodeling Tip:
Lay aside all the details of what you think God requires of you before He'll take up residence in your spiritual house. Spend time praying and giving God your heart—that's all He wants.

Day Four

Not a Craftsman

I'm not a very good construction worker. Seriously, you would not want to hire me. I don't like getting hot and sweaty. Hard hats ruin my hairdo, and steel-toed boots mess up my toenail polish. I'm not an exact person either; there abouts works great for me. That's why I am in awe of Moses, keeping the details straight and overseeing the craftsmen it took to complete the job. There was no compromise; he did exactly what God said to do.

My dad owned a construction company when I was growing up. I would occasionally go with him to check on different job sites. At a young age, I learned construction work is a very hard job. As I got older, I discovered the place for me was driving Daddy from job to job and staying in the cool air-conditioned truck as he checked on the different crews. I can still smell the oil, grit, and diesel that permeated that truck.

Jokingly, I can say I'm not a construction worker, but in reality, I need to be. If I'm a spiritual house, God's house, I will be in need of constant repair and restoration. You will be, too. Moses was in construction work. As Moses came down from Mount Sinai with the blueprints for the first tabernacle, he said, "All who are skilled among you are to come and make everything the Lord has commanded" (Exod. 35:10).

- Read Exodus 35:30 – 36:2. With what did God fill Bezalel? What did God give Bezalel and Oholiab the ability to do?

God laid out His plan for the tabernacle, a new tent of meeting, to replace Moses' old tent. God provided a plan, resources, and talents through individuals for every single detail to be carried out exactly as He had commanded. The Israelites might have messed up before, but they willingly gave and worked with their whole heart in this instance. The tabernacle began to come together beautifully.

God saw to it that everyone possessed the skills needed for construction. Bezalel was filled with the Spirit. He had the skill, ability, and knowledge in all kinds of crafts for the artistic designs prearranged by God. Bezalel, Oholiab, and others were given the ability to know how to carry out the construction plans as the Lord commanded. Not only that, they were also given the ability to teach others their trade.

God provided. He laid out the master plan with meticulous detail and saw to it that the Israelites were equipped with everything needed to carry it to completion. It is a perfect example of the following expression: "God does not call the equipped; He equips the called."

Such is the case in your spiritual life. You have been called to build a spiritual house, a dwelling place for Him, and He will equip you. You may not think you are a craftsman, nor that you have the skills or talents needed to build or renovate a temple, but God will provide. He will make a way, whether it is through friends, resources, or prayers.

If you believe Jesus is your Savior, God has imparted the same Spirit of John 7:39 within you.

- Write out John 14:15-21 in your own words. Who is the Counselor? Where does He live?

As God took Jesus back to the heavens, He left you the gift of His Holy Spirit. The same Spirit that provided the Israelites wisdom to build the tabernacle is the same Spirit that provides for your every need as you love and obey the commands of God. Through His Spirit, you can be a craftsman. He will provide you with skills and strength for carpentry and renovation work. As the Israelites stepped out in faith, trusting in God's Spirit, God provided the wisdom, abilities, and resources they needed.

- Do you think the carpenters and the skilled craftsmen knew the magnificence of the building they were constructing? Did they realize what they built would live on for generations through their legacy?

As the talented crew finished the tabernacle, it was prepared to travel. And travel it did as different kings ruled over the course of time. Years flew by, kings passed on, and the Lord's tabernacle moved from place to place. Finally it rested in the hands of King David.

King David revered the tabernacle: "When David was settled in his palace, he summoned Nathan the prophet. 'Look,' David said, 'I am living in a beautiful cedar palace, but the Ark of the LORD's Covenant is out there under a tent'" (1 Chron. 17:1 NLT). David definitely was a man after God's own heart. He realized he was living in the most incredible home, yet the Lord's house was out under a portable tent. David longed to build a permanent house, a temple, for the Lord. David drafted and planned out the most magnificent of structures to construct for the Lord.

God had never once complained about living in that tent as they traveled through the wilderness. This fact makes me think to myself, *Yikes, how dare I complain about the house I have?* God never grumbled about moving from place to place. Once again, I know I am guilty. He never asked for a beautiful house to be built in His honor. *O Lord, forgive me!*

Instead, God said He'd build His house through one of David's sons (1 Chron. 28:6, 7). When David died, Solomon took the throne as king (1 Kings 2:1). Solomon established his kingdom, and at Gibeon the Lord appeared to him in a dream saying, "Ask for whatever you want me to give you" (1 Kings 3:5).

- That statement is mind-boggling; however, it is still what God says to you. Write the following verses in your own words:
    Matthew 7:7-8
    Matthew 21:22
    Luke 11:10

Ask and you shall receive. Solomon could have asked for whatever he wanted. He could have asked for more square footage in a better neighborhood, a housekeeper, or a bigger bank account, but he didn't. He asks for something bigger: wisdom. That is wise! Observe how the Lord granted Solomon's request:

God gave Solomon wisdom and very great insight, and a breadth of understanding as measureless as the sand on the seashore. Solomon's wisdom was greater than the wisdom of all the men of the East, and greater than all the wisdom in Egypt. He was wiser than any other man. (1 Kings 4:29-31)

As the wisest man, Solomon begins construction on the temple, which was much larger than the tabernacle. This temple would be beyond beauty. Its details were to be suggestive of the tabernacle in the wilderness. And once again, God provided wisdom, materials, and skilled craftsmen to build the magnificent structure.

You might not be an architect, mason, or carpenter, but hallelujah, that's not what is required to build a temple today. The Spirit of wisdom that helped Moses, David, and Solomon is the same Spirit that will help you build your temple as you proceed from here. With God's Spirit, you can become who God created you to be. Oh, girl, you are a craftsman!

Today's Remodeling Tip:
Change your thought processes. Erase the words "I can't" from your vocabulary. You are a *can-do girl* because you have the Spirit of God living within you.

Day Five

A Passion for Your Place

I was so excited when my parents decided to build a house when I was in middle school. My dad, a real Mike Brady of the *Brady Bunch* television show, drew up the plans. The jobs were contracted out and our new house began to take form. It was exciting times. As the construction process proceeded, my dad would often receive phone calls in the middle of the night from the police or neighbors who were close to the construction site, alerting him that something had happened at the house.

Heading to the site, my dad would find where vandals had broken in, thrown a party, vandalized the property, or destroyed equipment. Seeing the project through to the end was tedious and became prolonged by the infringement of the hooligans. After each set back, it took shear determination and a passion to see the house through to completion.

- Write Psalm 69:9.

David definitely had a passion and an eager enthusiasm for God's house, as did Solomon. Over the course of hundreds of years, Solomon's Temple, which we studied yesterday, was vandalized, plundered, and destroyed. (Remember I'm not good at history. However, my husband said I needed a time reference.) The temple was rebuilt many times, but in 586 BC the Babylonian Army burned it and tore down the walls of Jerusalem. The temple seemed beyond repair (2 Chron. 36:18, 19).

The Lord, with such passion for His house, brought King Cyrus of Persia up in 536 BC to rebuild the temple at Jerusalem (2 Chron. 36:22, 23). "Then God stirred the hearts of the priests and Levites . . . to rebuild the Temple of the Lord" (Ezra 1:5, NLT). Soon co-workers began to arrive. Jeshua and Zerubbabel joined the construction crew with the same purpose in mind: to rebuild the temple. The Lord revealed to Zechariah that the reconstruction of the temple would assuredly come to completion.

I wonder if Zerubbabel was overwhelmed as he looked at the project ahead. Did he say, "There's no way. I'm not cut out for this job."? Praise God, Zerubbabel and the others took the steps needed and began the project. Zerubbabel didn't rebuild the temple in his own strength or might.

- Explain Zechariah 4:6 in your own words.

"Not by might nor by power, but by my Spirit." It was by God's Spirit that Zerabbabel was able to rebuild, just as Moses had relied on that same Spirit to build the tabernacle. You cannot build your spiritual home with your own power and might. It will take God's Spirit to provide the wisdom, talents, and resources you need. However, you have to take the first step. God will meet you there and begin building with you. He will provide the specifics as you continue to have a passion for your spiritual house.

Recall the New Testament story where Jesus went into the temple courts and found cattle, sheep, and doves being sold. His passion and zeal for that place cleared the area as He overturned tables (John 2:13-15). As the scene unfolds, "His disciples remembered this prophecy from the Scriptures: 'Passion for God's house will consume me'" (John 2:17 NLT).

- Write out John 2:17. What does this verse mean to you?
  What are you passionate about? What consumes you?

Your passion must be about God's house or God is not pleased. When Herod became King of Israel, he had plans to build a new temple, one that would be grander than the Jews had ever seen before. His extraordinary building plan gives insight to why he became known as Herod the Great.

Although Herod built the grandest of all temples, it was not a place that pleased God. It was a temple that glorified Herod, not God. Herod's temple stood less than one hundred years and has never been rebuilt.[3]

As you've looked over the course of history this week, you've seen how God invited others to build and to rebuild. You might be wondering why God allowed the temple to be torn down to begin with. Note: God didn't do the tearing down—man did.

I recently visited with a young woman who had been raped. She was having a hard time with why God allowed this to happen. She questioned how God could love her if He allowed this to happen. I assured her; I told her that God loved her, and He was not the one who raped her. God was the one loving her while sin was thrust upon her. God did not rape her; man did. Because God is a gentleman and gives us freewill, sin happens.

The temple was torn down by man, yet God continually raised people to rebuild so His glory would shine through. God comes to His people, the ones who have a passion for His house, and stirs their hearts to build a dwelling place for Him to inhabit so He can be close to them: "My dwelling place will be with them; I will be their God, and they will be my people" (Ezek. 37:27).

- Have you thought about the spiritual temple you are building? What passion pumps you up? A career? A home? A reputation? Does the building process leave you frustrated, tired, or even overwhelmed?

You might have to build, rebuild, and renovate one hundred times over, but never give up. Keep your passion alive. There will be days you're frustrated, and you'll wonder if it is worth it. Don't give up! Just as you saw God continually beckon His people to set up a home in which He was proud to dwell, He will continually summon you to build and reside with Him. When you have a passion for His place, it affects your whole being. Your relationships will be transformed, the way you treat your body will be modified, and old addictive habits will be dismissed.

A dear friend gave me a gift for Christmas, *The Word on the Street.*™ This is a rendition of the Bible in which the author expresses John 2:17 in these words: "Passion for Your place pumps me up."[4] Isn't that the same overwhelming zeal we should feel for God's temple?

If you are passionless today, ask God to give you a hunger for faith and a passion that pumps you up! It's OK—you can get excited and show enthusiasm. This generation, myself included, has been emotionless far too long. Seriously, this is an awe-inspiring plan. Think about it: God wants to live with you. *Hello!* God wants to live in you. *Woo Hoo!*

Full of wonder and emotion, I've found myself weeping and on my knees in worship this week. My eyes and heart have been opened as I've jumped into studying the temple. It's as if I've been transported back to temple times, and now I get it.

What truly touches my soul is the fact that God wants to dwell and abide in me and you. All through time, He has provided ways to dwell among us. Makes you just want to shout, *"PTL!" Praise the Lord.* My educated mind knows this; however, I think this week my heart finally got it.

What an overwhelming feeling to know He loves you so much that He, the creator of the galaxy and stars, wants a continual, personal relationship with you. Oh my, the Creator of the moon, stars, zebras, oceans, platypus, and the common housefly wants to know you. Not only that, but next week we'll see that He wants to live within the same body as you. You can't get much closer than that! Mercy, this is simply mind-boggling.

O Lord, pump us up. Give us a passion and enthusiasm for Your house. Let us build a holy and spiritual house for You, and only for You. Holy Spirit, help us see it to completion. Thank you for wanting to dwell with us. Amen.

Today's Remodeling Tip:

On a scale of 1 to 10, pinpoint your passion for God's house. Does this mark coordinate with where you spend your time, money, and resources? If not, reinvest in your passion.

Week Two
A Guest or a Resident?

*W*hen I was growing up, I moved once to a different neighborhood. I lived in the same city for twenty years. I was very comfortable in my small, countrified neighborhood. However, that feeling of comfort was stripped away at the age of twenty when I got engaged to a man in the U.S. Army. We were planning our wedding to take place as soon as he graduated from flight school. As he was finishing up his program, we waited everyday for his orders. These orders would give us our first duty assignment as a married couple.

When the phone call came, we were excited, thrilled, and a little anxious. They were sending us to Frankfurt, Germany. My lands, what were they thinking? We were young and surely didn't need to be that far from home. But Uncle Sam ordered it, so we packed and went.

It was strange to live in a foreign country. I couldn't speak German, couldn't read their road signs, and had no idea of how to get around. This was 1982, and the native residents weren't too happy about having Americans around. I truly felt like an unwelcomed guest in this foreign country. I never felt accepted or welcomed.

I will say it was a great land to visit. We traveled and saw amazing sights. I saw first hand all those magnificent castles and monuments that I was supposed to have learned about in high school.

Our three year tour passed quickly, but each day I longed more and more for home. My prayer for you this week is that you will realize that no matter where you are, you are home if God dwells within you.

Day One

Location, Location, Location

*W*hat's in a location? A lot! Moving every couple of years while my husband was in the military was quite stressful. We learned a helpful realtor could make the moving experience less stressful. A common saying each realtor shared was "location, location, location."

Over the centuries, moving has become more complicated, or has it? Surely Moses and the "campers" searched for the best possible location as they moved from place to place. They might not have looked for good schools, athletic clubs, and great restaurants, but I bet they looked for a prime location. Surely the women would have recommended a place close to a river so it wasn't so far to walk for laundry day. I think some might have suggested a flat piece of land so they didn't roll out of their tents as they would lie down to sleep. Property and location certainly do go hand in hand. So it is with our spiritual house:

Didn't you realize that your body is a sacred place, the place of the Holy Spirit? Don't you see that you can't live however you please, squandering what God paid such a high price for? The physical part of you is not some piece of property belonging to the spiritual part of you. God owns the whole works. So let people see God in and through your body. (1 Cor. 6:19, 20 Message)

- From the verse above, name the property. Name the location. Who owns the property? Who paid for the property?

You are God's property, His prize possession. Don't take this to mean that you're just a piece of property, like a master thinks of a slave. No! You are a highly esteemed piece of property, a possession so sacred and valuable that God Himself—the Master Builder, Artist, and Designer—has come to dwell within you.

God picked the perfect location, took up residence, and put His Son in charge of you, His property: "But Christ, as the Son, is in charge of God's entire house. And we are God's house, if we keep our courage and remain confident in our hope in Christ" (Heb. 3:6 NLT).

You are a perfect piece of property, sitting in the most valuable location. Are you with me? I see you shaking your head thinking, *Nope you don't know me. I'm unworthy, used, and cheap. I'm definitely not a valued piece of anything. If you only knew my past; I consider myself more like a piece of trash than valuable property.*

Those are lies, dear one. They are mistruths from the one who comes to kill, steal, and destroy, the one who acts much like the Big Bad Wolf in the *Three Little Pigs* (John 10:10). This wolf, Satan, knows how perfect and priceless your property is, and he will do anything to ruin and destroy it.

- What lies is the evil one telling you about your property? Do you feel you are constantly treated like the world's garbage and everybody's trash (1 Cor. 4:13)?

Because you are priceless, God bought you with the most valuable currency: His Son's blood. He wasn't scrounging for foreclosures. He wasn't looking for a project. He was looking for you. He signed the deal the day He purchased you with His Son's blood. He paid the highest price imaginable and guaranteed it with a deposit, His Holy Spirit:

It's in Christ that you, once you heard the truth and believed it (this Message of your salvation), found yourselves home free—signed, sealed, and delivered by the Holy Spirit. This signet from God is the first installment on what's coming, a reminder that we'll get everything God has planned for us, a praising and glorious life. (Eph. 1:13, 14 Message)

God notarized the deal. He signed for you, sealed you with the Holy Spirit, and delivered you from the evil one. You must be an exquisite, valuable, and precious piece of property. You weren't a good deal, a bargain, or a steal. You cost Him his everything– His one and only Son. There's no need to worry about location, location, location. You are it! You can take that to the bank—guaranteed (2 Cor. 1:22).

All those years I followed my dad around checking out construction sites, I picked up a bad habit. Whenever Daddy was out and needed to make a quick note so as not to forget something, he'd pull out his pen and write it on his hand. I soon found myself doing that same thing and still do to this day. But this isn't anything new. Notice how God marks us:

*But for now, dear servant Jacob, listen— yes, you, Israel, my personal choice. God who made you has something to say to you; the God who formed you in the womb wants to help you. Don't be afraid, dear servant Jacob, Jeshurun, the one I chose. For I will pour water on the thirsty ground and send streams coursing through the parched earth. I will pour my Spirit into your descendants and my blessing on your children. They shall sprout like grass on the prairie, like willows alongside creeks. This one will say, 'I am God's,' and another will go by the name Jacob; **That one will write on his hand 'God's property.'** (Isa. 44:1-5 Message, emphasis added)*

- Write Isaiah 44:1-5 in your own words. Substitute Jacob and Israel with your own name.

I like the idea of writing "God's property" on your hand. As a matter of fact this mom would love to write it across my two daughters' foreheads for all the boys and the world to see. Why discriminate against my son? He could use a new tattoo as well. Maybe we'd all view each other differently if we were reminded constantly that we are God's property.

You are His property, whether you feel like a brand new house, an old fixer upper, or a torn down hut. He longs to reside at your place on location.

Today's Remodeling Tip:

Kick your feet up and take a break from fixin' up. Open the door and allow God in. You're property is perfect for His presence.

Day Two

Taking Up Residence

$\mathcal{M}$y mind is still processing the thought that I am God's house. You and I house the Lord of Lords and King of Kings. *Whoa!* The same God that created Adam and Eve, parted the Red Sea, and made water spring from rocks lives here, today, in us. If we could truly comprehend that thought, we'd certainly be paralyzed in awe of His wonder and the responsibility we have to house THE LORD.

> *But if God himself has taken up residence in your life, you can hardly be thinking more of yourself than of him. Anyone, of course, who has not welcomed this invisible but clearly present God, the Spirit of Christ, won't know what we're talking about. But for you who welcome him, in whom he dwells—even though you still experience all the limitations of sin—you yourself experience life on God's terms. It stands to reason, doesn't it, that if the alive-and-present God who raised Jesus from the dead moves into your life, he'll do the same thing in you that he did in Jesus, bringing you alive to himself? When God lives and breathes in you (and he does, as surely as he did in Jesus), you are delivered from that dead life. With his Spirit living in you, your body will be as alive as Christ's! (Rom. 8: 9-11 Message)*

God has moved in, taken up residence, and now abides in you. When your schedule is busy and hectic, He is there living in you. When you are relaxing, troubled, sick, or hurting, He lives in you.

Through your roles, daily routines, and responsibilities, He lives in you. You are His house, and He is home.

- What comes to mind as you realize your physical body houses the Lord of all creation? If you can't comprehend that you are the spiritual house of God or if that seems foreign, let me ask: Have you asked Him to move in and claim residence within you?

1 John 4:15 reads, "If anyone acknowledges that Jesus is the Son of God, God lives in him and he in God." If you haven't taken that step of faith and acknowledged Jesus as the Son of God, do that now by praying this prayer: *Dear God in heaven, come into my heart and fill me with Your presence. I proclaim that Jesus is Your Son. I believe He was crucified, died, and was buried, only to rise again to live with You. Thank you, Lord, for loving me so much that You sent Your one and only Son just for me. It's through His most precious name and blood that I pray and claim Him as my Savior. Amen.*

If you just claimed and accepted Jesus as your Savior for the first time, I strongly urge you to contact your minister and a Christian friend to let them know of your decision. They will be able to lead you to the next step. If you are feeling a tug at your heart, don't stop here. Let your heart ask, just as the people asked Peter and the other apostles, "'Brothers, what shall we do?' Peter replied, 'Repent and be baptized, every one of you, in the name of Jesus Christ for the forgiveness of your sins. And you will receive the gift of the Holy Spirit'" (Acts 2:37, 38).

What a precious gift to receive the Holy Spirit, to have the God of the universe live within you and set His tabernacle up within you. John 14:15-20 says it this way:

If you love me, you will obey what I command. And I will ask the Father, and he will give you another Counselor to be with you forever— the Spirit of truth. The world cannot accept him, because it neither sees him nor knows him. But you know him, for he lives with you and will be in you. I will not leave you as orphans; I will come to you. Before long, the

*world will not see me anymore, but you will see me. Because
I live, you also will live. On that day you will realize that I
am in my Father, and you are in me, and I am in you.*

That scripture leaves me squirming because I'm not the best
housekeeper, nor do I have the best spiritual house. I truly feel like
a fixer-upper most of the time. But the Lord didn't come to dwell
in the most expensive or well kept temple; He came to dwell within
His people. God didn't ask for terrazzo floors, wrought iron trim-
ming, or gold lamp posts. He doesn't ask for the size zero body or
the perfectly shaped smile. Just as He was willing to dwell with
Moses in a dusty old tent with hard, cracked, dirt floors, He is eager
to dwell within me—just as I am.

Your residence is everything to God. Your heart and body is His
tabernacle—His dwelling place. God longs to tabernacle with you,
not at a vacation resort or a winter chalet.

- Do you see yourself as the prime location for God?
  Why or why not? If your residence is unoccupied,
  maybe it's time to let Jesus in.

God's love amazes me. He doesn't care what kind of shack,
beaten up old house, or temporary housing you live in; He wants
to take up residence with you. As God calls out, He hopes you'll
say, "Here I am, Lord. Come and reside in me."

Today's Remodeling Tip:
Identify the thoughts that steal your joy and leave your house
feeling empty. Once identified, train your mind to stop the thoughts
in their tracks before they contaminate your home.

Day Three

The House Guest

When I was very young, my favorite cousin lived two hours away. It wasn't very often that I got to see her, but when her family came to town, it was an exciting time. Let me clarify—it was exciting, except for the house cleaning. Mom would have my brother, sister, and I all busy with our chores so the house would be picked up for company. I could have cared less about our household duties. I just wanted my cousin to be there.

We lived very far out in the country, and there was a very long, rocky driveway that led to our house. After I completed my tasks, I would ride up and down that long driveway on my banana seat bike, waiting for my cousin. I couldn't wait to spend time with her.

Do you consider guests coming to visit a blessing or a curse? When house guests let you know they are coming to visit ahead of time, you have the opportunity to get your house in order. But sometimes that can be an overwhelming chore; there are beds to strip, sheets to wash, bathrooms to clean, floors to vacuum, and furniture to dust.

You might be thinking, *That's nothing! You should be at my house when company comes to visit. Not only do I have to clean, but I have to make sure all the movies that are inappropriate are put away, throw out the magazines others would find offensive, and hide all the liquor bottles.*

I have fallen into that trap many times myself. I didn't want company coming into my "real life" and seeing the "real me." The things I knew were not acceptable (because they were sin) I would have tried to hide. Cigarettes, alcohol, magazines—you get the picture. Then there was the day someone popped in unannounced. Unannounced! You can imagine the panic that struck the minute the doorbell rang. Your heart starts pumping, and your mind is racing to what you need to cover up or pick up. You scurry through the house like a mad woman on your way to the door. I call this the "flight of the bumble bee."

- Does the above scenario resonate with you? Are there things you are hiding and covering up?

It is strained and awkward any time you are covering up or hiding things that you know aren't right. I often wonder why we put so much pressure on ourselves to pretend to be something or someone we are not. You've said it and so have I: "No one is perfect." It has become so cliché that we don't take it to heart and find freedom in the words. Now, this sentiment doesn't give us the go-ahead to sin. But, remember that sin is sin, whether it is out in the open or hidden. Why are we hiding sin to protect our perfect appearance?

I love the story of Zacchaeus. He knew he was a sinner, yet he didn't do the "flight of the bumble bee" or stall when Jesus said, "Zacchaeus. . .I must stay at your house today" (Luke 19:5).

- Read Luke 19:1-10. Write down what you think Zacchaeus was feeling as he went to see Jesus that day. What emotions must have flooded Zacchaeus' mind as Jesus said, "I want to be a guest in your home today"?

Let's read the story together:

When Jesus came by, he looked up at Zacchaeus and called him by name. "Zacchaeus!" he said. "Quick, come down! I must be a guest in your home today." Zacchaeus quickly climbed down and took Jesus to his house in great excitement and joy. But the people were displeased. "He has

gone to be the guest of a notorious sinner," they grumbled.
(Luke 19:5-7 NLT)

Spend some time visualizing this scene. In my mind, I see Zacchaeus at a point in his life where he was questioning and wondering about this man named Jesus. Was Jesus really the Messiah? Did He really know everything about everyone?

I personally think Zacchaeus' conscience and the spirit of God was at work within him. As a tax collector, he knew he had swindled absurd amounts of money. There was enough for him to live in luxury and still give the government their portion. But I wonder if Zacchaeus came into this wealth as part of a power trip to try to prove himself.

He was quite short in stature, and I'm sure he heard about it growing up. Do you have things in your past that you've heard about over and over? Are you short or overweight? Were you from a dysfunctional family or a very successful one? Zacchaeus might have had all the wealth and power he could dream of in that time, but he knew he was missing something in his life. He knew there had to be more and maybe—just maybe—this Jesus was it.

- Are there things that drive or have driven you to excel? Do you have a need to prove yourself? If so, are you sensing there must be more? Is it time you climb up a sycamore tree?

Just when Zacchaeus thinks, *There must be more to life than this,* he climbs that Sycamore tree, and there is Jesus. To prove to Zacchaeus that there was more to life than material gains by swindling others, Jesus says, "Zacchaeus, come down now. I'm coming to your house today—this minute."

Notice Zacchaeus' response. He comes down quickly with great joy and excitement and takes Jesus to his house. Zacchaeus didn't run ahead so he could put away his elaborate décor or expensive wines. No, he was pretty sure Jesus knew him – the "real" Zacchaeus. Jesus had called him by name.

- Look back at Luke 19:5-6. Jesus calls you today, just as He did Zacchaeus. Do you greet Jesus with such great joy and excitement? Are you pleased to have Him come to your home and see the "real you"?

My heart cries out, *Lord, forgive me for not wanting to invite you into my home because I'm not perfect enough.* Jesus knows me and my struggles. He wants to come and dwell within me to help me in those areas, yet I hold Him back because I think I'm not cleaned up enough. There are so many lessons to glean from this wee, little man. Paul puts it perfectly, "Therefore, there is now no condemnation for those who are in Christ Jesus" (Rom. 8:1). I pray that no matter what makes you feel condemned, unclean, or unworthy, you never let that come between you and Jesus.

So many times I have thought my real self wasn't good enough to approach Jesus. I've also met many women who have confessed the same insecurity. Relax, knowing that you're not the only one who has ever felt this way. Remember, God knows you, calls out to you, and hopes you will joyfully and excitedly take him into your house, your heart—His home—today. You don't need to clean up first, just invite him in to be a guest.

Today's Remodeling Tip:
Dust your furniture. Think about the things that leave you feeling useless and envision them being cleaned away.

Day Four

Abide With Me

*J*esus only asked to be a guest in the home of Zacchaeus; however, He asks much more of us. He doesn't want to come in for a temporary visit or an overnight stay; He wants to live, dwell, and abide with us.

However, we'd prefer Jesus to be the house guest rather than the resident. It is relatively easy to clean up our home for a few hours, but making a life-long change takes effort. Actually, I think it is easier to be a guest in Jesus' home. I can go through my life not thinking very much about Jesus dwelling within me, but I show up to church on Sundays and visit with Him. I've easily fallen into this trap at times in my life.

Sunday was visitation day. I'd get "cleaned up" Sunday mornings with my best clothes, finest smile, and most excellent attitude and arrive at church as a guest in Jesus' home. I'd sing the worship songs and pray, but deep down somehow, I felt out of place. I'd leave there at noon, having visited with my Lord for an hour, but still feeling disconnected from His presence. I knew something wasn't right.

- Is Sunday visitation day for you? Have you experienced times like this in your life? What emotions engulfed you?

In Luke 7, Jesus enters Capernaum where He is confronted by leaders in the Jewish community. They wanted Jesus to come heal a sick servant. Jesus heads off with them, and while He is still far away, the captain sends friends to tell him, "Master, you don't have to go to all this trouble. I'm not that good a person, you know. I'd be embarrassed for you to come to my house, even embarrassed to come to you in person" (Luke 7:6-7 *Message*).

Being embarrassed for Jesus to see the real you is nothing new. There are many who would feel unworthy to have Jesus enter their homes. But Jesus doesn't look at your home or your problems; He looks at your heart.

You have someone living in you who understands you, accepts you, and who can help you. That help springs forth not only by visiting church weekly and hoping to see Jesus there, but also from realizing that Jesus is within you and remains with you. He waits for you to realize He is in you every moment of every day, not just at the church building.

- Does realizing Jesus is with you every moment calm your anxious heart and quiet your fears, or does it make you more anxious?

While I was growing up, I took piano lessons for years, and every Thanksgiving we had the Hymn Festival. Oh, how I dreaded it! This was a recital where every student had to memorize two hymns and then perform them on the specified date. Invariably, I would always get the hymn *Abide with Me*. Although it wasn't my favorite hymn to memorize, the words have stuck with me over the years:

Abide with me; fast falls the eventide;
the darkness deepens; Lord, with me abide.
When other helpers fail and comforts flee,
help of the helpless, O abide with me.[5]

John 15:4 (KJV) puts it best, "Abide in me, and I in you." God cannot say it more clearly. My prayer for you is what Paul prayed for his Ephesian friends: *"I pray that out of his glorious riches he may strengthen you with power through his Spirit in your inner being, so that Christ may dwell in your hearts through faith. And I pray that you, being rooted and established in love, may have power, together with all the saints, to grasp how wide and long and high and deep is the love of Christ"* (Eph. 3:16-18).

Thankfully, God made a way and provided for us to feel comfortable with Him residing within us. That provision was made through Jesus, His one and only Son, who not only died for us but also knows every pain we feel. Jesus tells us in John 14:1-3, "Do not let your hearts be troubled. Trust in God; trust also in me. In my Father's house are many rooms; if it were not so, I would have told you. I am going there to prepare a place for you. And if I go and prepare a place for you, I will come back and take you to be with me that you also may be where I am."

What an incredible gift! As the Lord of the Heavenlies lives within us, there is no reason to feel like an outsider or to be shamed as a worthless sinner. Jesus knows you. He knows your struggles, just as He knew Zacchaeus' struggles. After visiting with Zacchaeus, Jesus says in Luke 19:9,10, "Today is salvation day in this home! Here he is: Zacchaeus, son of Abraham! For the Son of Man came to find and restore the lost" (*Message*).

The Son of Man does not want to dwell within you to condemn and judge you. No! He longs to reside within you to restore the lost, hurting, wounded, broken, and sinful places in your heart. He doesn't want to be a guest for one night or a visitation requirement once a week. He wants to be with you every moment. Open your heart and let Him in. He comes to heal your life and break the chains that hold you down.

As my heart tries to grasp the gravity and depth of God placing Himself within me to dwell and abide, I know my words do not convey the awesomeness I feel. My only prayer is you begin to feel that overwhelming awe, too.

Today's Remodeling Tip:

Speed clean your house. Get rid of anything you would not want others to see. Never allow those things back in your house.

Day Five

Tabernacle with Us

   As we studied last week, it was God who directed Moses to build the tabernacle so that He could dwell with His people. But what about today, the times in which we live? Acts 7:48, 49 tells us that "The Most High does not live in houses made by men. As the prophet says: 'Heaven is my throne, and the earth is my footstool. What kind of house will you build for me?' says the Lord. 'Or where will my resting place be?'."

- Write Acts 17:24 in your own words. What does this convey to you?

   Just as in the Old Testament, we tend to see the church building or temple as the place where Jesus lives. That was true up until the time of Jesus' glorious return to heaven. However, through His work and the gift of the Holy Spirit, God no longer dwells in a physical holy place. John 1:14 tells us that "The Word became flesh and made his dwelling among us."

   Literally, the word *dwelt* here means tabernacled—to reside and abide. God took up His residence among us, more specifically, within us, some two thousand years ago. Now, rather than God being someone to be feared because of His consuming glory, Jesus is here to take away our sin and pain. Jesus can now feel our hurts and know, first hand, the temptations facing us. He understands all our emotions and the struggles that leave us feeling inadequate and undeserving. If you are feeling lonely, beaten down, afraid, or tempted, Jesus understands.

For the last two weeks, we've studied God's house or tabernacle. We now have some serious questions to ask ourselves. Glance back to Acts 17:24.

- What kind of house are you building for God? Are you relying on human hands to renovate your home? Does God live in temples built by hands?

We live in such a busy world, and each day, our to-do list seems longer than the hours in the day. Unless we make a concerted effort to think about the kind of house we are building, we will let our habits dictate our blueprints and plans. Some of those habits could use a little challenging and tweaking. Some should be swept out of our lives completely.

Before Christ made His way in the world, God sent John the Baptist to go before him and pave the way. This led others to think that John was the Messiah. In Luke 3:16 (*Message*), John intervenes:

I'm baptizing you here in the river. The main character in this drama, to whom I'm a mere stagehand, will ignite the kingdom life, a fire, the Holy Spirit within you, changing you from the inside out. He's going to clean house—make a clean sweep of your lives. He'll place everything true in its proper place before God; everything false he'll put out with the trash to be burned.

- Who is the one who will ignite the kingdom life and place the Holy Spirit within you? What will the Spirit do?

There is something priceless about housing the Spirit of God. His Spirit makes sure you have the best life, if you put your trust in Him. With your faith, He cleanses your house from the inside out. That is the only way to truly come clean. Anyone can throw on a coat of paint or straighten up the landscaping to look good, but renovating the interior is where the work will give its greatest payoff.

- Write out Proverbs 14:1. Who builds her house?

Solomon tells us, it is the wise woman who builds her house and the foolish one who tears it down. Don't you think it would have been helpful if he would have included a little check list right there? If you do this, this, and that, then you are well on your way to being a wise carpenter. As you begin next week's lessons, we will dig in and define "wise" principles using Biblical blueprints.

You've already determined the best location for the temple and found out that you're it—God's property. It's time to be the best of the best as God tabernacles within you.

Dear Heavenly Father, Thank you for loving us so much that You sacrificed your Son to buy us. Thank you for sending the Holy Spirit as a guarantee that You are with us always. Thank you for wanting to dwell within our physical being, Lord. Amen.

Today's Remodeling Tip:

Paint your fingernails. Let this serve as a reminder that anyone can throw on a coat of paint to look good, but true change only comes through renovating your heart.

Week Three
Change is Here

One of the coolest things my daddy did as he designed our home was to make a small replica of the house. He made the house to scale, but it was a much smaller version. Every room, door, and window was put in the correct place. As he built the replica, my brother, sister, and I would watch in amazement as we saw our new house take shape. I think our fighting over bedrooms began at this phase.

The wisdom my dad had in planning ahead was flawless. He not only had a replica of the house, but he also reproduced the articles to go in the house. He wanted to make sure this dream home he was building for our family was exactly what we wanted. He even made little-bitty appliances, furniture, and beds that we could move around to verify that we had the space we needed.

Before my dad ever broke ground to start building, he knew exactly what our new house was going to look like, inside and out. That is a valuable lesson for our spiritual houses as well. Douglas Lurtan says, "When you determine what you want, you have made the most important decision in your life. You have to know what you want in order to attain it."[6]

My prayer for you this week is that you begin praying for wisdom and take the first step needed to begin renovating your house with the finished project in mind.

Day One

Build with Wisdom

*D*o you wonder what steps you need to take to renovate your house? You might be thinking it is a lost cause because you feel like an old fixer-upper, but Christ says you're never beyond renovation. Today, let's dig a little deeper into making the calculated choice to build our homes with wisdom.

Solomon had wisdom. He was the wisest man and gives us examples that we should follow. Recall his story:

> *That night God appeared to Solomon and said to him, "Ask for whatever you want me to give you." Solomon answered God, "You have shown great kindness to David my father and have made me king in his place. Now, LORD God, let your promise to my father David be confirmed, for you have made me king over a people who are as numerous as the dust of the earth. Give me wisdom and knowledge, that I may lead this people, for who is able to govern this great people of yours?" God said to Solomon, "Since this is your heart's desire and you have not asked for wealth, riches or honor, nor for the death of your enemies, and since you have not asked for a long life but for wisdom and knowledge to govern my people over whom I have made you king, therefore wisdom and knowledge will be given you. And I will also give you wealth, riches and honor, such as no king who was before you ever had and none after you will have. (2 Chron. 1:7-12)*

Solomon went on not only to rebuild the temple with great wisdom, but he also provided us with thoughts about wisdom throughout the book of Proverbs:

> *By wisdom a house is built,*
> *and through understanding it is established;*
> *through knowledge its rooms are filled*
> *with rare and beautiful treasures.*
> *(Prov. 24:3-4)*

> *The fear of the LORD is the beginning of knowledge,*
> *but fools despise wisdom and discipline.*
> *(Prov. 1:7)*

> *By wisdom the LORD laid the earth's foundations,*
> *by understanding he set the heavens in place.*
> *(Prov. 3:19)*

> *Know also that wisdom is sweet to your soul;*
> *if you find it, there is a future hope for you,*
> *and your hope will not be cut off.*
> *(Prov. 24:14)*

- Using the verses above, write out your definition of wisdom. Name the ways your spiritual home will become stronger with wisdom.

Wisdom accomplishes much. Using wisdom and understanding to plan ahead, you will be saved from disasters. The Lord laid the earth's foundations with wisdom. Just think if He had not planned out how to create the earth. What a disaster it would have been. Reading through the creation story, one easily sees how our God is a planning God. Thank goodness, or Adam might have arrived on the scene with nothing to eat!

The fear of the Lord is where wisdom begins. Believe it or not, the wise old owl has nothing to do with it. Wisdom is not something that sits atop a tree and sings out, "Hoo Hoo." It is something to be feared and to be asked for, just as Solomon did. Fear is not being afraid of God; rather, it is revering Him.

- Look up these verses and write your definition of fearing the Lord:
    Proverbs 3:7
    Proverbs 8:13
    Proverbs 14:16
    Proverbs 16:6

Fearing the Lord is turning away from evil, pride, arrogance, recklessness, and perverse speech. It also incorporates being self-less and realizing my thoughts are not God's thoughts or ways. It is so easy for me to think I have all the answers, and before I know it, I'm functioning out of my own pride and recklessness. I could use a double dose of wisdom, just as God gave Solomon. If you are thinking the same thing, there is hope for both of us: "If any of you lacks wisdom, he should ask God, who gives generously to all without finding fault, and it will be given to him. But when he asks, he must believe and not doubt, because he who doubts is like a wave of the sea, blown and tossed by the wind" (James 1:5, 6).

If you are overwhelmed and lacking the wisdom you need to renovate your spiritual house, it is time to ask God to help you see the first step to take. James makes it clear that God will give generously when you ask sincerely, not doubting that He will answer. Feel free to recite this prayer as often as needed while renovating:

Lord, I come before you this moment asking for an extra measure of wisdom and grace. I thank you in advance for the wisdom You will send and the ways You will work within me. Please forgive me of my past failures to spruce up Your home. Help me forgive myself and let go. Guide me into Your understanding and wisdom to make lasting changes that will glorify You. Let your light shine through me and open my eyes to see Your wisdom as I go from here. Amen.

Today's Remodeling Tip:

Memorize Proverbs 24:3-4: "By wisdom a house is built, and through understanding it is established; through knowledge its rooms are filled with rare and beautiful treasures."

Day Two

Survey the Land

I enjoy looking through books that have house plans. My mind wanders and tries to envision my family living in each of the design layouts. The thoughts that cross my mind are, *Nope, that kitchen is too small. There is not a place for the baby grand piano. Need to move the kid's rooms away from the master bedroom.* I'm sure my "dream" home looks different from yours, just as my spiritual house is different from yours.

Having a clear picture of the end result will help you create your dream home. Some of you probably have known what kind of a spiritual house you've wanted for awhile, but you've never set out to accomplish the makeover. Are you looking to modify your habits, release the anger, or reshape your body? I'll admit making a heart and a lifestyle change is not easy. It is easier to slap on a coat of paint and cover up the mess. But instead of fixing up the outside, this is where you have to put on your steel-toed boots and hard hat and work on the inside. With that said, let's put on our boots and hard hat. Today, we are going to do some digging. Let's begin with the end in mind.

You have a style of living that is unique to you, just as I do. That is how it is with God's house—your heart. Your heart has strengths that mine does not have. We each have weaknesses, but chances are, they are different. All of those factors need consideration as we begin to renovate God's house.

- Think about the type of character qualities you'd like to gain or be rid of by the end of this study and in the months to come. Make note of what you'd like not to see in your spiritual house: smoking, cussing, and bitterness. Or, make note of the qualities you would like to add: more peace and knowledge of the Lord. How would you like to look, act, and function at the end of these six weeks?

Listen up! Hear Joshua ask you, just as he asked the Israelites at Shiloh who were looking to receive their inheritance, "How long will you wait before you begin to take possession of the land that the LORD, the God of your fathers, has given you? Appoint three men from each tribe. I will send them out to make a survey of the land and to write a description of it, according to the inheritance of each" (Josh. 18:3, 4).

How long will you wait? Those words echo within me. How long will you wait to begin the diet that will lead to a healthier you? How long will you wait until you get serious about your overspending? How long will you wait before you begin a daily relationship with God? How long will you wait before you respect your husband?

How long before you understand you can't take possession of who you want to be until you are responsible for your actions? How long will you wait before you begin?

- If Joshua were to send men to survey your lifestyle and habits, what would they report back? Write a description of what they would find.

Surveying your life is important. You need to know what you are facing and what your challenges are before you set out for renovation. Maybe you have skeletons in your closet that need to be cleaned out. Maybe you have someone you need to forgive. Maybe your mind constantly replays abusive and negative words others have thrown at you. Maybe your self-image thermostat is set too low. Knowing the struggles and weaknesses you face is necessary to living the life you'd like to live.

Living in this hectic world, we are so busy taking care of everyone else that finding time to be alone is a challenge. There is not a quiet moment to survey our own lives. We have to know where we are to be able to conquer the challenges ahead as we renovate God's house. We have to know our reality.

- What is the reality of your spiritual house? What needs to change?

If you haven't surveyed your property yet, you need to keep your hard hat and boots on until you do. Please don't move on until you have spent time surveying your life and know your current reality. It's not fun taking a good, hard look at yourself, but it is a must.

I'll enjoy a cup of cool water while I wait on you to finish your day's work of diligently digging. You need to know your reality before you step out to create your dream home. You have done an awesome job surveying and excavating. Now you can take off those boots, gloves, and hard hat.

Today's Remodeling Tip:

Dig up the weeds in your flowerbeds. As you pull up each unwanted, wild plant, ask yourself, "How long will you wait until you begin the changes necessary to be who you want to be?"

Day Three

Count the Cost

*I*t's amazing how putting something down in writing frees you. I hope you found your surveying exercise a liberating job yesterday. Alright, I'm sure it wasn't fun as you went through the process, but now that you have it down on paper, you can easily see what you need to work on. Once it is down in black and white, there is no arguing with it. However, I've heard many women say that's why they don't want to write those changes down. It's hard to look at reality.

You've conquered the first step to having that dream home you want, and you'll be glad to know, there will be no need for hard hats today. If you've ever built a house or been with anyone going through the process, you know there is a lot that goes into the project before the lot is even cleared. Today, you'll begin by estimating the cost: "Is there anyone here who, planning to build a new house, doesn't first sit down and figure the cost so you'll know if you can complete it? If you only get the foundation laid and then run out of money, you're going to look pretty foolish. Everyone passing by will poke fun at you: 'He started something he couldn't finish'" (Luke 14:28-30 *Message*).

- Restate the above scripture in your words. Do you find this applicable in your life? Are you a planner? Do you plan with the end in mind? Have you started something before and not finished?

I'm sure you realize that if you are going to build or renovate, you need to count the cost first. You might be wondering, *What cost?* All change comes with a cost. It is so easy for us to say we want to be free of the bitterness we harbor or we want to lose weight, but those are just words. There's a time when we have to act on those convictions so they can become our new reality. The Holy Spirit that God left within us is the one convicting us of the things we need to remodel. The Spirit is nudging us to clean out the closets and knockout old habits: "It is clear to us, friends, that God not only loves you very much but also has put his hand on you for something special. When the Message we preached came to you, it wasn't just words. Something happened in you. The Holy Spirit put steel in your convictions. You paid careful attention to the way we lived among you, and determined to live that way yourselves. In imitating us, you imitated the Master" (1 Thess. 1: 4-6 *Message*).

- Who puts steel in your convictions so you can imitate the Master?

Our steel-toed boots will only get us so far, but the Holy Spirit can help us through it all to conquering those convictions. The strength you will need to turn words into actions and actions into a victory will be found through the Holy Spirit. Glance back to yesterday's lesson where you listed what you'd like to see in your spiritual house.

Proverbs 4:7 says, "Though it cost all you have, get understanding." It is a grueling process to look at yourself and see why you've failed in the past or why you are failing now. It's a process you won't enjoy, but you will gain wisdom and understanding from taking the time to take a thorough and honest look at yourself.

I'm sure most of us have tried to patch up our lives before or to trouble shoot one area. Maybe you succeeded. If you accomplished the task, think about what brought it to completion. Were you determined, regardless of what you faced? Did things get so bad that you had no choice but to change? Were you diagnosed with a health condition which drove you to change?

On the other hand, there are those areas you've tried to change and you've failed. You've heard the famous saying: "If at first you don't succeed, try, try again." However, if you continue trying the same thing the same way, you won't get anywhere. Remember the definition of insanity? Insanity is doing the same thing over and over and expecting different results.

- List the areas in your life that you've tried to change without success. Why did you fail? Did you not have steel in your convictions? Were others not supportive of your change? Did you really want to change?

You haven't listed the reasons you failed to set the stage for your future. No, you listed them to learn from them! When you know your struggles, you can be on the lookout for them as you go forward; you can learn from your mistakes of the past. There's no time to look backwards or dwell in the past. It's about moving on with Jesus to be who God created you to be:

On the road someone asked if he could go along. "I'll go with you, wherever," he said. Jesus was curt: "Are you ready to rough it? We're not staying in the best inns, you know."

*Jesus said to another, "Follow me." He said, "Certainly, **but** first excuse me for a couple of days, please. I have to make arrangements for my father's funeral." Jesus refused. "First things first. Your business is life, not death. And life is urgent: Announce God's kingdom!" Then another said, "I'm ready to follow you, Master, **but** first excuse me while I get things straightened out at home." Jesus said, "No procrastination. No backward looks. You can't put God's kingdom off till tomorrow. Seize the day." (Luke 9:57-62 Message, emphasis added)*

I've proclaimed I want to be like Jesus and follow His ways; however, there have been times when I've suffered from the *but* syndrome like the two followers above. I've said, "Lord, I want to live a life made over for You, *but* this week is going to be tough. There are people I'll be with and situations I'll be in that will make this impossible." Can you relate?

Or maybe we're more like the first person Jesus encountered on the road. We're all words. We never even get to the *but* stage. Our convictions sound good, and we've voiced them; however, we don't have intentions of following through. I can't tell you the number of times I've said I was going to the gym and never made it there.

Wherever you find yourself, take the time to consider the cost. Will the cost motivate you to avoid certain temptations, people, or food? Will it cost you more time in prayer to release the bitterness and anger you've bottled up? Will it cost you time in preparation and scheduling? Call upon God's Spirit to put determination in your britches as you move on from here. It will be worth the cost.

Hear Jesus say, "No procrastination. No backward looks. Seize the day."

Today's Remodeling Tip:

No backward looks. Write a letter to yourself explaining who God created you to be and why. Refer back to this letter often as a reminder of who you are becoming.

Day Four

Ready for Change

$\mathscr{A}$s I write this study, we are in the process of remodeling our master bathroom. This has been an ongoing project for what seems like years. I find remodeling interesting; even when you are in the talking phase, it actually seems like you are really working on something.

My husband, Curt, and I have talked about this project off and on. When he'd get ready to proceed, he'd ask if I was ready. Invariably, it was always bad timing. There would be get togethers, parties, or speaking engagements on the calendar, and it just wasn't a good time.

After months of this delay, Curt finally said, "When you are ready, you let me know." He was tired of talking and ready for me to make the decision to move ahead with our plans. It was time to take action to implement the change.

- Read John 5:1-9. Write down your initial thoughts.

The Pool of Bethesda, according to the Bible, had a tradition. An angel would move the waters at certain times and heal the sick. For the healing to take place, the lame and crippled, who lived homeless and helpless, would call out to a passerby to help them into the pool when the water was stirred. It was here that Jesus healed a man who had been lame for thirty-eight years.[7]

I remember the first time I read this story. I was flabbergasted by the first words out of Jesus' mouth: "Do you want to get well?" *What?* The answer seemed pretty apparent to me. Besides, didn't

Jesus already know the answer?

Notice the man's response, though. He doesn't shout out a resounding, "Yes!" or even a sarcastic, "Duh?" He automatically lists the reasons he hasn't been able to make it into the healing pool. I'm guessing he had probably used these excuses before: I have no one to help me. People look right passed me. I am paralyzed.

Do any of those excuses ring a bell with you? Or maybe you have your own set of excuses, just as I do: *I'll start tomorrow. Just one more won't hurt me. No one can see what goes on behind closed doors. I've tried before and failed. I don't have the strength.*

Jesus might not be calling to you, "Do you want to get well?". But, can you hear Him? He is asking, "Are you sure you want to renovate your spiritual house? Are you positive you want to make those changes?"

Making those changes we talked about yesterday will require more than words and hope. Change requires action. Although Jesus' question seems a little insincere, it is loaded with a challenge. Do you *really* want the changes you are talking about? Making changes will bring change.

- Write out some changes that would have been made in the cripple's life once he was healed.

The man who had been crippled for thirty-eight years was no longer going to be able to lie by the pool and beg for help. Instead, he would need to become an active person in society: working for a living, paying for food, and bathing himself. Did he really want to be healed? Life would definitely be different. It would be something he had never experienced before. You can bet he was about to be thrown out of his comfort zone, if he answered "yes."

- How long have you been crippled or broken? Do you need time to think about if you really want to change?

I want to change, and I'm tired of praying the same prayer over and over. However, without any action or fortitude behind my words, God cannot move. He might be stirring my heart like He did the waters at Bethesda, but if I don't jump in and take action, He cannot work a miracle. Jesus told the cripple to get up, take his mat, and walk. Once he acted upon Jesus' commands, he was healed.

- Jesus is probably not giving you the same instruction that he gave the cripple. However, take a moment and listen. What is He telling you? What action is He requiring of you?

As we rap up, let's continue to ponder over Jesus' words. I've got a song in my head. I hope you recognize it. It's from one of my favorite shows of all times, *The Brady Bunch*. This song, *Time to Change*, will surely date me:

Well its time to change
You've got to rearrange
Move your heart to what your gonna be.
sha na na na na na na na, sha na na na na na[8]

Today's Remodeling Tip:
Walk through your house and change all the light bulbs that need to be replaced. Recite over and over, "It's time to change!" as you conquer this task.

Day Five

Home is Where Your Heart Is

ou've heard the saying, "Home is where your heart is." There is such truth to those words. Over all the years that Curt and I moved from place to place in the military, I can only think of one place I did not care for. My heart ached as I couldn't stand where we were. I wanted to leave, and yesterday would have not been soon enough. As I shared this with my mom, she responded, "Alene, home is where your heart is." I thought, *My point exactly! This doesn't feel like home, and I don't want to live here.*

After I had time to digest her words, I realized I had a heart problem, not a home problem. It was a nice house we were living in, but my heart was having an attitude of its own. Proverbs 4:4 says, "Lay hold of my words with all your heart; keep my commands and you will live." I can assure you I was not keeping God's commands, and His words were not in my heart. Instead, my heart was filled with anger and selfishness.

Let's see what God says our heart and home should be filled with.

- Look up each scripture, and write it in your words. Make note of what God intends your heart to be filled with.
   Proverbs 3:1-2
   Proverbs 14:30, 33
   John 14:27

If home is where our heart is, there is much we can learn about what we need to fill our hearts up with. God is looking for a heart that is full of righteousness, understanding, and blessings. A heart should be secure and a place of rest. There will be an all-surpassing, unexplainable peace when your heart is focused on God.

God also sends direction for things to rid our hearts of in 1 Samuel 7:3: "And Samuel said to the whole house of Israel, 'If you are returning to the LORD with all your hearts, then rid yourselves of the foreign gods and the Ashtoreths and commit yourselves to the LORD and serve him only, and he will deliver you out of the hand of the Philistines'." God reminds us to rid ourselves of all foreign gods. In other words, anything that captivates our attention more than God needs to go.

- Look up the following scriptures and make note of what we should rid ourselves from:
    Ezekiel 18:31
    Ephesians 4:31
    Colossians 3:8-9

It is impossible to have a peaceful home, no matter where you live, when you are constantly in a rage or brawl. God tells us to sweep these things out of our hearts because they can take root and cause greater destruction. Anger, bitterness, malice, and filthy language pollute our homes. It's time to free our hearts of the offenses we've committed and get a new spirit.

In *God Calling,* one of my favorite devotional books, A.J. Russell sums up the thought that our home is where our heart is: "As one on earth who loves another says, 'Where you are is home,' so it is in relation with Me. Where I am is My home—is heaven. Heaven may be in a sordid slum or a palace, and I can make My home in the humblest heart."[9]

Home is where the heart is, and God's home is in our heart. It doesn't matter if we live in the ghetto or Bel Air, in a great big house or a little bitty dump. God doesn't look at the physical structure; He looks at our heart. We often end up unsatisfied with where we are living, and that is because this world is not our home (1 Pet.

2:11). Instead of turning to God to find our comfort, joy, and peace, we turn to the world around us that screams our homes aren't big enough, strong enough, or even green enough.

As long as you are with the One you love the most, you are home. Are there things you need to rid yourself of so you can once again feel at home in your own house? Once your heart is dusted and free of worldly clutter, you will see more clearly.

Take some time before we begin our next week's lesson to examine yourself. Block off some time to do a home inspection. Write out what needs to change, what needs to go, and summarize the price you need to pay. Whatever the price, it is worth it to make yourself at home in your own home once again. If you need some help, come on over, because *Mi Casa Es Su Casa*!

Heavenly Father, thank you for dwelling within us. Lord, convict us of the adjustments that need to take place and put steel convictions behind those changes. Draw us nearer to you, Lord. Amen.

Today's Remodeling Tip:
  Memorize Proverbs 4:23: "Above all else, guard your heart, for it is the wellspring of life."

Week Four
The Carpenter

*A*fter our first three years of married life in Germany, we returned stateside to Alabama. Curt was in the Army, stationed at Fort Rucker as an instructor pilot, and we were ready to live the American dream.

We had lived in military housing those years in Germany and decided we wanted our own place. We looked everywhere around Fort Rucker and found nothing that suited our fancy. We finally found a place down an old, country, winding road where an engineer was building new homes on half acre lots.

This was a home that the architect had already designed and the carpenters had begun constructing. It was easy to see what the house would look like because the foundation was lain and the wall frames were up. We were so excited. We were twenty-three years old and going to own our first home.

The coolest part about this adventure was we were going to get to pick out the entire interior to match our style. We quickly learned that fixtures, flooring, and wallpaper could be quite expensive. Nonetheless, it was an incredible journey. It was a treat to see that framed structure eventually take a style and become a home.

The Architect has already laid the foundation and put up wall frames in your spiritual house. My prayer for you this week is that you let the Carpenter in and begin designing your dream home.

Day One

He Stands at the Door

*I*magine Happy Home Housekeeping pulling up to your house and knocking on your front door. You hadn't called them, so you curiously open the door. They ask if you'd like your house cleaned. You answer, "Of course!" Only a crazy woman would say no at this point. Happy Home Housekeeping continues to tell you that they are running a great deal. Not only will they clean, but they have others with them that can help you renovate.

You stand in disbelief. "What? Excuse me?"

"Ma'am, we're here today, knocking on your door, giving you the opportunity to have your house cleaned and renovated. Will you accept our offer?"

What are your initial thoughts? Are you one who would run and clean up the house before you'd allow Happy Home Housekeeping in to clean? That's alright if you are. I have a friend who has a housekeeping service come in every week, and the night before they arrive, she does the "flight of the bumble bee." She cleans before they clean. Crazy!

On the other hand, some of you might be thinking, *Sure, come on in and stay awhile. My house needs so much cleaning, organizing, and renovating, you will definitely need more than one day to help me out.* I can relate more to the second scenario than the first. Either way, you are probably thinking the Happy Home Housekeeping scenario seems a little far-fetched. As we relate it to our spiritual house, you'll soon realize it isn't.

- Write out Revelation 3:20. Who is knocking at the door?

Jesus stands outside the door of your heart, knocking. It's time to open the door and let Him come in. He wants to come in and be your friend. Are you going to open the door?

He is knocking at the door of your heart. I have a feeling you can hear Him and you've sensed Him there for sometime. Don't let this moment pass you by. It doesn't matter if you've just accepted Jesus or if you've been a believer all your life. Maybe you've grown cold and apathetic in your spiritual walk, and you're wondering where Jesus is. He's at the door, waiting for you to ask Him back in. Maybe you have wandered away, but He hasn't. He still stands at the door knocking.

Don't cautiously creep to the door. Run to it! Let Him in and enjoy His sweet fellowship. More than anything, He'll make it apparent He wants to be your friend. He'll be the one to help you renovate, remodel, and make the changes you've thought about and listed last week. He'll help you see the project through to completion.

- What is stopping you from opening the door? Are you troubled over what Jesus will see on the inside? Or, are you excited to let Jesus in so you can absorb His presence?

Dear one, open the door and let Him in as He has asked. Are you thinking you'd rather God break down the door, rush in, and save you? He could, but He won't. He gives you free will to choose Him and the life He has to offer. Therefore, He stands on the other side, outside your heart, knocking continually. Hopefully, you'll rush to greet him and let Him in.

Girls, Jesus doesn't go only to the wealthy neighborhoods and knock there. He knocks everywhere. He is in every town, city, and suburb, knocking. He knocks no matter what the income, education, or qualifications. He knows no boundaries and has no limits as to how far His love will extend.

Jesus stood beside the waters of Bethesda as the Great Physician. He now stands outside your door as the Master Designer. Remember what a fantastic job Moses did by following God's exact directions for building the temple. Jesus is even a better draftsman, engineer, and designer: "But Jesus deserves far more glory than Moses, just as a person who builds a house deserves more praise than the house itself. For every house has a builder, but the one who built everything is God" (Heb. 3:3, 4 NLT).

God built the tent of meeting, tabernacle and temple through His people so that He could be close to them. Today, He stands outside your door, longing to come inside and rebuild, restore, and renew your heart—His house—through His Son Jesus.

His invitation is simple, "Open the Door."

Today's Remodeling Tip:

Sweep off your front porch. Think about Jesus coming to visit. Imagine opening the door for Him to enter.

Day Two

No Hammer Needed

     *A*s you open the door of your heart and see Jesus standing there, you are anxious about seeing the Holy Son. Maybe you expect Him to be beaming bright lights, and you can't look because it will hurt your eyes. That's the way you've seen Him in all the pictures. But quickly you do a double take because Jesus doesn't look anything like the images you've seen. He's not glowing, frail, or skinny. You take notice that He's muscular, toned, and darker than you imagined. He's a carpenter.

- Describe how you picture Jesus. Do you visualize him as a carpenter? Describe a carpenter's strengths.

Jesus' family and those in his hometown could only see Him as "just a" carpenter (Mark 6:3). But Jesus was much more. His training as a carpenter not only gave him the physical strength to care for others, but it also gave him a heart to build and renovate. He was skilled and precise. His gifts found in human form undoubtedly included the ability to be creative and craft something new from raw materials. That heart was definitely exhibited for all mankind as He went to the cross for our sins, knowing that if we understood and accepted Him, He could create something new within our hearts. Jesus' passion to create has led Him to assist you in renovating yourself to become a new person (Eph. 4:20-24).

- Have you ever been referred to as "just a"? When you were growing up, were you "just a girl" or "just a tomboy"? Maybe later in life you became "just a divorcee, single mom, lawyer, or a homemaker." How did the references hurt or help who you are today?

Jesus knew he was more than just a carpenter. He let the comments roll off his back as He knew He was doing what He was called to do. I have to admit that this is not an easy thing for me to do. Sticks and stones may break your bones and words DO hurt! However, Jesus continued on, despite the insensitive references. He was here to create something new within the lost and sinful of the world, and nothing derailed Him.

- Write out 2 Corinthians 5:17.

Since you have accepted Christ and opened the door of your heart to let Him in, you are now a new creation. The old has gone. The wounded heart that's been hurt by cutting remarks, the poor self-image that was created after years of abuse, and the angry disposition lingering after battling addictions can all be created anew.

Paul wrote it beautifully in Ephesians 4:20-24:

But that's no life for you. You learned Christ! My assumption is that you have paid careful attention to him, been well instructed in the truth precisely as we have it in Jesus. Since, then, we do not have the excuse of ignorance, everything— and I do mean everything—connected with that old way of life has to go. It's rotten through and through. Get rid of it! And then take on an entirely new way of life—a God-fashioned life, a life renewed from the inside and working itself into your conduct as God accurately reproduces his character in you. (Message)

Jesus entered your heart to take away the old and replace it with a creative, new way of looking at things. He came to reveal the rotten and ask that you throw it out. He wants to fashion a God-centered life in you. You are probably thinking, *I knew it! The carpenter came in, and now he's ready to take the sledgehammer and wrecking ball to my very core.* Seriously, that's not so! Hear me out.

If you'll take another good look at Jesus as He stands before you, you'll notice He didn't enter with His hammer. Jesus, the carpenter, entered your spiritual house without any tools. He entered as your friend, ready to help you remodel your life from the inside out. He won't beat you into a new creation. Instead, He asks that you be willing to let Him work within your life. No hammer is needed, just a gentle nudging:

> *So here's what I want you to do, God helping you: Take your everyday, ordinary life—your sleeping, eating, going-to-work, and walking-around life—and place it before God as an offering. Embracing what God does for you is the best thing you can do for him. Don't become so well-adjusted to your culture that you fit into it without even thinking. Instead, fix your attention on God. You'll be changed from the inside out. Readily recognize what he wants from you, and quickly respond to it. Unlike the culture around you, always dragging you down to its level of immaturity, God brings the best out of you and develops well-formed maturity in you. (Rom. 12:1-3 Message)*

God will bring out the best in you through Jesus, the carpenter. It doesn't matter if you think you're "just an ordinary person," He wants you to give it to Him. If you're . . .

just a busy body,

just a saleswoman,

just a mom,

just a wife,

just a problem-child,

just a doubter,

just a hurt soul or

just a dreamer . . .

listen to Jesus. He knows you are much more, and He'll create something beautiful from within. He won't beat you into submission. He won't trick you into change, but He will gently lead you through the process of restoration.

He left the hammer at the cross. Hallelujah!

Today's Remodeling Tip:

Memorize Revelation 3:20: "Here I am! I stand at the door and knock. If anyone hears my voice and opens the door, I will come in and eat with him, and he with me."

Day Three

A Solid Foundation

*A*s Jesus steps into your home, you notice He begins to look at the ceiling and the walls as if He's inspecting them thoroughly. Your heart starts racing as you ask what He's looking for. He explains that if there is a weak or faulty foundation, He'll be able to tell because there will be very small cracks in your structure. Today we'll see why there's no need to renovate unless the foundation is sound and secure.

The foundation of your home is the most important structure. *Boring, I know.* But it's the building block upon which everything else is built. If there's a faulty foundation, there is, or will be, a broken down structure.

- Rewrite in your own words the story of the wise and foolish builders found in Matthew 7:24, 25. How important is the foundation?

If you grew up in Sunday school you probably remember the song that goes along with the scripture:

The wise man built his house upon a rock, and the rains came tumbling down.
The rains came down and the floods went up, and the wise man's house stood firm.
The foolish man built his house upon the sand, and the rains came tumbling down. The rains came down and the floods went up, and the foolish man's house went SPLAT!

That little ditty is a reminder to build your house upon the Lord Jesus Christ.

Years ago, Curt and I began to see hairline cracks in our ceiling and in our tile floor. Asking around, we found out this could be because our foundation was splitting. We were told that if we didn't deal with this, it could lead to massive problems in the future. We had experts come out, and it was confirmed that we needed foundation repair. We chose a company, and they quickly began repairing, restoring, and stabilizing our foundation. We learned through this process that although our house was built upon solid ground in the beginning, it had been improperly cared for and the foundation had weakened.

- Can you relate this to your spiritual house? Do you see hairline cracks running through your foundation? Maybe those cracks come in the form of lies, doubts, bitterness, or even a lack of forgiveness. List them, and let's begin repairing your foundation, one step at a time.

Jesus is your foundation. If your house is not built upon Him, it will collapse. Jesus Christ himself is your chief cornerstone that everything else is built upon (Eph. 2:20-22).

- Write out 1 Peter 2:5-7. Who is the spiritual house? Who is the precious cornerstone? What benefits are there in trusting and believing?

We become living spiritual houses as the living Christ comes to dwell within us. When we put our trust and faith in Him, we won't be ashamed and rejected because of our hair-line cracks. Instead, we will live life renewed and restored:

God is building a home. He's using us all—irrespective of how we got here—in what he is building. He used the apostles and prophets for the foundation. Now he's using you, fitting you in brick by brick, stone by stone, with Christ Jesus as the cornerstone that holds all the parts together. We see it taking shape day after day—a holy temple built by God, all of us built into it, a temple in which God is quite at home. (Eph. 2:19-22 Message)

Having a firm, secure, and solid foundation is key to renovating your spiritual house. Without that base to lay all else upon, everything will crumble. Hopefully, you took the time earlier in this lesson to inspect your foundation. If you saw a fracture, I hope that you took the time to think over it and see where it might have come from.

When Curt and I realized we hadn't cared for our foundation properly, we learned the steps we needed to take so the problem didn't get worse. We had to provide a constant moisture level for the soil around our foundation, and we got rid of big roots growing under and close to our foundation. Our spiritual foundation is much the same. Once we realize we have foundational cracks, we need to trim the big roots and begin providing constant moisture to the soil.

- What kind of big, useless roots might be growing up underneath your foundation? Could guilt shame, unbelief, or prayerlessness be wrecking your foundation?

Maybe the root that needs to be dug up is greed, or the love of money (1 Tim. 6:10). Perhaps the root is bitterness (Heb. 12:15). There are many things we allow to damage our foundation.

Curt and I also noticed that it wasn't just the trees in our yard whose roots were damaging our foundation; our neighbors' trees were also causing harm. Their tree roots had grown clear up under our foundation and were causing our cracks too. Sometimes in our spiritual house, other people's habits, decisions, and actions send roots that begin producing hairline fractures in our foundation. We must always be on guard against the damage roots can cause.

To secure your foundation, you need to continually and earnestly seek God. When your heart has such a thirst for Him that you can't stand it, you can be assured your foundation is solid and built with Christ as the cornerstone:

Or, to put it another way, you are God's house ... Let each carpenter who comes on the job take care to build on the foundation! Remember, there is only one foundation, the one already laid: Jesus Christ. Take particular care in picking out your building materials. Eventually there is going to be an inspection. If you use cheap or inferior materials, you'll be found out. The inspection will be thorough and rigorous. You won't get by with a thing. If your work passes inspection, fine; if it doesn't, your part of the building will be torn out and started over. But you won't be torn out; you'll survive— but just barely. (1 Cor. 3:9-15 Message)

You don't want to barely survive. You want to thrive in your spiritual house. To secure your foundation, you must learn to transform the way you think. Behind everything you do is a thought. Each behavior is motivated, at its very root, by a belief: "Nothing shapes your life more than the commitments you choose to make. Your commitments can develop you or they can destroy you, but either way, they will define you."[10]

Don't let your thoughts, commitments, or bad habits destroy you. You might say, "Well, I've got willpower." Girl, willpower is not enough. It will produce a short-term change, but it creates constant stress upon your foundation because you haven't dealt with the root cause. Find those roots that are putting stress upon your foundation, dig them up, and secure your foundation.

Change always starts at the foundation with a solid commitment. To be a spiritual house, you must rely on Christ as He is your foundational cornerstone. Build your house on the Word of God so it will last forever.

Today's Remodeling Tip:

Inspect your home's walls, ceiling, and floors for small hairline cracks. If any are noted, find out if they are related to foundational troubles.

Day Four

Light of the World

$\mathcal{A}$s Jesus walks through your home, he quietly asks, "Can you brighten the light in here?" Jesus obviously feels it isn't light enough. Your mind starts racing with questions of why He needs more light. After a brief moment of awkward silence, Jesus says, "I am the world's Light. No one who follows me stumbles around in the darkness. I provide plenty of light to live in" (John 8:12 *Message*).

Jesus, not the local power company, is the power you need for adequate light: "For God, who said, 'Let light shine out of darkness,' made his light shine in our hearts to give us the light of the knowledge of the glory of God in the face of Christ. But we have this treasure in jars of clay to show that this all-surpassing power is from God and not from us" (2 Cor. 4:6, 7).

Jesus often refers to himself as *the light* and asks us to walk in *the light* (1 John 1:7). Do you wonder what *the light* is?

- Read John 3:20-22. How do you come into the light?

Jesus tells us that those who do evil cannot come into the light. But those who live by truth are in the light. What truth are we to live by? "Jesus answered, 'I am the way and the truth and the life. No one comes to the Father except through me'" (John 14:6). If you live with Jesus, you live with truth and light.

Are you thinking, *This sounds great, but I have no idea how to brighten the light of my heart and the truth of my soul.* Do you remember the childhood song "This Little Light of Mine?" Let me sing it for you (sorry for any flat notes):

This little light of mine,
I'm going to let it shine,
let it shine all the time,
let it shine.

Jesus puts it another way:
No one lights a lamp and puts it in a place where it will be
hidden, or under a bowl. Instead he puts it on its stand, so that
those who come in may see the light. Your eye is the lamp of your
body. When your eyes are good, your whole body also is full
of light. But when they are bad, your body also is full of dark-
ness. See to it, then, that the light within you is not darkness.
Therefore, if your whole body is full of light, and no part of it
dark, it will be completely lighted, as when the light of the lamp
shines on you. (Luke 11:33, 34)

If you know the truth, you aren't going to hide it. You're going
to hold it out, loud and proud, for all to see. However, if you are
hiding something dark—secret sin or buried bitterness—it will be
hard (actually impossible) for your light to shine fully.

- From the scripture above, what is the lamp of your
  body? Why do you think this is so?

I love *The Message* translation of Luke 11:33, 34:

No one lights a lamp, then hides it in a drawer. It's put on
a lamp stand so those entering the room have light to see
where they're going. Your eye is a lamp, lighting up your
whole body. If you live wide-eyed in wonder and belief, your
body fills up with light. If you live squinty-eyed in greed and
distrust, your body is a dank cellar. Keep your eyes open,
your lamp burning, so you don't get musty and murky. Keep
your life as well-lighted as your best-lighted room.

- Describe a life lived wide-eyed in wonder and belief. What does a life that is squinty-eyed in greed and distrust look like?

The purer we are in Christ, the more His light and His truth are able to shine through us. The cleaner we are, the freer we are to put our lights out for all to see. It's no wonder Jesus asked, as he entered our home, if we could turn more lights on. He is the purest light there is; we all lack in comparison. Even if we think we are living the purest of lives, with our lights beaming bright, I think we'd be surprised by how much influence the world has on how brightly our lamps shine.

Some days I can be a good housekeeper. I do a pretty good job of keeping things picked up, but when it comes to those details like dusting the blinds, scrubbing the baseboards, or cleaning light fixtures—*sigh*—I fail.

Eventually, when I notice the lights becoming dim due to the amount of dust on the fixture, I relent and take a day for cleaning those glass globes. This tedious chore is a process: take the glass globes off, dust away the cobwebs, soak the globes, scrub the dust out of the globes, dry the globes, and then put them back on the fixture. But the best part is when I turn on the lights, and goodness, I really have bright lights again.

It wasn't until I cleaned the globes that I realized how much that dirt was blocking the light from shining through into my home. I can tell you that freshly cleaned fixture globes shine so much brighter. This is like our spiritual home. When our hearts are corroded with the things listed above, our home becomes dull: "The light of the righteous shines brightly, but the lamp of the wicked is snuffed out" (Prov. 13:9).

David writes in Psalm 101: 2, 3, "I will walk in my house with blameless heart. I will set before my eyes no vile thing." We should be able to walk into our sanctuaries with a blameless heart. We've created the atmosphere in our homes and are living in truth with Jesus. But it is what's in our hearts that sets the tone of our homes.

- Read all of Psalm 101. List the vile things which you should refuse to give a second look. (View different Biblical translations for an eye-opener.)

It amazes me how hard it is to stay pure and bright in this world. There will always be influences and situations that will dampen our light. In the scripture above, I'm reminded of the influences my eyes see on television. All of what David mentions is seen every night on prime time TV, and it is also seen daily in real life: those who are faithless, those with perverse hearts, those who slander and have haughty eyes. People who practice deceit, speak falsely, and plan evil walk by us every day.

I'm reminded today that not only do I need to rid myself of the vile things that darken my Spirit of light and truth, but I should also guard my eyes from the same as I go about my day. Jesus is my only power source. He is the light of my home.

Because He knows your light affects others, Jesus asks you to turn on the lights in your house: "You are the light of the world. A city on a hill cannot be hidden. Neither do people light a lamp and put it under a bowl. Instead, they put it on its stand, and it gives light to everyone in the house. In the same way, let your light shine before men, that they may see your good deeds and praise your Father in heaven" (Matt. 5:14-16). No wonder Jesus wants your lights shining brighter; it causes others to praise His Father in heaven. It's time to turn on the lights and rid yourself of darkness.

Today's Remodeling Tip:

Clean all your light fixtures. Wash away the dirt and grime. Notice and enjoy the brighter lights.

Day Five

Living Water

*Y*ou are amazed you are beginning to see things brighter and clearer. Jesus was right when He said the lights could be a little brighter. You are lingering in His presence when you hear Him ask you for a drink. Once again, your mind wonders as to what you should serve the King of kings. As you head to the kitchen, you remember the story of the Samaritan woman:

> *Jesus, tired as he was from the journey, sat down by the well. It was about the sixth hour. When a Samaritan woman came to draw water, Jesus said to her, "Will you give me a drink?" (His disciples had gone into the town to buy food.) The Samaritan woman said to him, "You are a Jew and I am a Samaritan woman. How can you ask me for a drink?" (John 4:6-9)*

I can relate to the Samaritan woman. I find myself saying, "How can I do this for you, Lord, when I'm just an ordinary girl?" I don't think I'm good enough that Christ would use me. I don't feel significant enough that Christ would ask something of me. Nor do I believe that Christ counts me valuable enough to live within me. It is a constant battle guarding against those thoughts and realizing, *Yes, Christ loves me!*

- Put yourself in the Samaritan women's place. Write what you would be feeling.

The story continues in verse ten:

Jesus answered her (the Samaritan woman), "If you knew the gift of God and who it is that asks you for a drink, you would have asked him and he would have given you living water." "Sir," the woman said, "you have nothing to draw with and the well is deep. Where can you get this living water? Are you greater than our father Jacob, who gave us the well and drank from it himself, as did also his sons and his flocks and herds?" Jesus answered, "Everyone who drinks this water will be thirsty again, but whoever drinks the water I give him will never thirst. Indeed, the water I give him will become in him a spring of water welling up to eternal life." The woman said to him, "Sir, give me this water so that I won't get thirsty and have to keep coming here to draw water." (John 4:10-15)

If we truly understood and knew the gift of God, it wouldn't be Jesus asking us for a drink; instead, we would be begging Christ for a drink of that living water. The Samaritan woman realizes she wants this living water, but she wonders where in the world she'll get it. She immediately thinks Jesus is referring to the well. But Jesus answers, "Everyone who drinks this water will be thirsty again" (vs. 13).

Water is so essential to our being. Our bodies are made up of eighty percent fluid. Stop drinking water and see what happens. Coherent thoughts vanish, skin grows clammy, and vital organs wrinkle. In fact, your Maker wired you with thirst—a "low-fluid indicator." Let your fluid level grow low and watch the signals flare. Dry mouth. Thick tongue. Achy head. Weak knees. Deprive your body of necessary fluid, and your body will tell you.

Deprive your soul of spiritual water, and your soul will tell you. Dehydrated hearts send desperate messages. God does not want you to live with any of the following: hopelessness, sleeplessness, loneliness, resentment, irritability, insecurity. These are warning signs, symptoms of a dryness deep within.[11]

Have you ever felt parched, dry, and barren within? I have, and I felt helpless, alone, and disconnected. I think the Samaritan woman might have felt this way. Reading John 4:17, 18, you see she was living with a man and had already had five husbands. She was relying on men to fill the thirst, the void in her life. She was desperately seeking something.

- List the things you rely on to quench your thirst. Do they help?

We cover our thirst in many ways: men, alcohol, church activities, food, shopping, and pills. However, we will never be satisfied until we get a good, long, tall drink of something that fully quenches.

- Read John 7:37, 38. Describe what will fully quench your thirst.

It's time to quit sipping the dirty well water. Jesus says if you come to Him to drink, He will fully satisfy. He satisfies through His spirit that lives within you. No worldly fix will gratify your desire for more. You will continually thirst for more unless you are filling up on living water.

In the desert, David knew what it was to thirst, but more important than his craving for H2O was David's thirst for God: "O God, you are my God, earnestly I seek you; my soul thirsts for you, my body longs for you, in a dry and weary land where there is no water" (Ps. 63:1).

It has been an awesome week as we've invited Jesus into our homes and realized that He is here moment by moment as our foundation, power source, and living water. Handing Jesus a refreshing glass of ice water, you hear Him say, "If you are thirsty, come! If you want life-giving water, come and take it. It's free!" (Rev. 22:17 CEV).

Dear Heavenly Father, thank you for knocking at the door of our hearts until we answer. Lord, forgive us when we forget you are our true power source and the water we should thirst and crave. Keep our minds fixed on You living within us. Amen.

Today's Remodeling Tip:

Make sure you drink eight glasses of water to replenish your bodily fluids. As you drink, remember it is Christ, the living water, who hydrates your soul.

Week Five
Put Your House in Order

$\mathcal{O}$ur last duty assignment before we retired from the military was to Corpus Christi, Texas. We were excited to be back on old, familiar stomping grounds. We made all the arrangements, coordinated with the moving and real estate companies, and we were able to move into our new home the minute we arrived in town.

Our three kids were all elementary age, and it seemed the boxes we'd hauled were more numerous than ever before. We unloaded for days. We worked tirelessly for over a month. Finally, the day came when the last box was unpacked and gone. We were home.

The next weekend we left town for a trip to Houston where my son was receiving an award from NASA for an international contest he'd entered. We had a great weekend—until the cell phone rang. It was our neighbor, whom we barely knew, saying that there was water running out the sides of our house, as well as down our driveway. Great! We asked that he turn the main water valve off and told him we'd be home in four hours.

Our minds were racing to what we were going to see when we arrived. Those four hours seemed like forever! In the late hours of the night, we pulled onto our street, and when we were close enough to see our house, we had to bust out laughing. The neighbors had figured out how to get inside our home. They had all our furniture out in the front lawn and the carpets ripped up. It was quite the sight. All I kept thinking was, *I just put the last box away.*

It was time to put our home back in order again. My prayer for you this week is that you'll be challenged to see new ways to put your home in order.

Day One

Carried to the Table

fter drinking a big gulp of living water from Jesus' cup, He asks if you'll join Him at the dining room table. You find your mind thinking, *Oh no, Lord, not the dining room table. I don't feel worthy enough to commune, eat, and visit with you in such a way!* Jesus leads the way, even though you hesitate.

Hesitating, you realize you are wounded, broken, and lonely. If you are to sit across the table from Jesus, you know He's sure to notice every flaw and hurt. You pause for what seems like eternity, and the next thing you know, Jesus is beside you lifting you up into His arms, carrying you to the table. He seats you at the table beside him, a place you feel you don't belong.

- Would you hesitate to dine with Jesus? If so, what would hold you back? If not, what do you long to share?

I love the Old Testament story of Mephibosheth. In 2 Samuel 9:1-13, David asks Ziba (I love that name) if there is anyone left from the family of Saul. Ziba answers that there is Mephibosheth, a son of Jonathan's, who is lame in both feet. King David doesn't lose a minute; he sends for him:

"Don't be frightened," said David. "I'd like to do something special for you in memory of your father Jonathan. To begin with, I'm returning to you all the properties of your grand-father Saul. Furthermore, from now on you'll take all your meals at my table." Shuffling and stammering, not looking

him in the eye, Mephibosheth said, "Who am I that you pay attention to a stray dog like me?" (2 Sam. 9:7, 8 Message)

Jesus calls out the same message to you and me in our weakness: "Don't be frightened." He knows we make ourselves vulnerable when we sit down to eat and commune with Him, but He wants us to trust Him enough to share. I find myself questioning, just like Mephibosheth: "Who am I that you pay attention to me?" I might not be lame in both feet, but I assure you, I have my own handicaps and weaknesses that I battle day in and day out. No matter what our circumstances are, the King summons us to the table to meet with Him.

- Read Psalm 23:4-6. Write what the Lord speaks to you.

No matter what dark valley, circumstance, or brokenness you are walking through, Christ not only summons you to the table, but He has also prepared the table and wants to meet you there. He calls and hopes you'll come.

Think of all the ways you use your dining room table. I'm sure we can all name a million ways. But hopefully your top two ways are similar to mine. I use my table mostly for eating with family and friends and for visiting with those who stop by. That's exactly why Christ invites us to His table: to visit, commune, and eat in His presence.

In Week One, we studied how the temple came to be. As God laid out the blueprints for the tabernacle, He also made it very clear what was to be in the interior. There were specific plans for a table.

- Read Exodus 25:23-30. Describe the table and how it was to be used.

A beautiful table it was. A table I'd love to see with my own eyes. *Where's Samantha from Bewitched when we need her?* The Bread of the Presence was to be on this table at all times, and it was located in the Holy Place within the tabernacle. It was foreshadowing of the Bread of Life that was to come.

Hear Christ explain the ultimate meaning of the bread:

I am that bread of life. Your fathers did eat manna in the wilderness, and are dead. This is the bread which cometh down from heaven, that a man may eat thereof, and not die. I am the living bread which came down from heaven: if any man eat of this bread, he shall live for ever: and the bread that I will give is my flesh, which I will give for the life of the world. (John 6:48-51 KJV)

The bread represents Christ, who is the Bread of Life, the bread from Heaven. It represents His purity, being made of the finest flour without additives. It represents the sufficiency of God's provision, the bounty of the table He has prepared for us in His presence. And it represents the lives we are to lead as those set apart to God. A pure and undefiled life. One growing relationship with the Lord. A life that continually feeds on this amazing delicacy.[12]

To feed from this awesome meal, we must be willing to meet Jesus at the table everyday. It is there He will change our heart from broken, wounded, forgotten, and alone to blessed and overflowing.

Are you living off fresh bread and the wisdom you gain by communing with Christ at the table daily, or are you hoping the stale bread you consumed last week will hold you over? If you were to share with others what you have consumed, would you describe your fare as fresh, pure, and satisfying or stale, dull, and unfulfilling?

Oh, girl, may you consume the fresh, wholesome bread of His presence and a living relationship with Jesus. How do you do this? You abide. You live. You consume. You sit and visit with the one who carried you to the table.

Today's Remodeling Tip:

Clean off your dining room table. Find some time to meet Jesus there. Be refreshed by the Bread of His Presence.

Day Two

Come and Sit

$\mathcal{A}$re you feeling the peace of Jesus' presence as you take a moment at the table and commune with Him? He carried you there, not to savor some fast food or a quick meal, but to enjoy fellowship with you. Sit and be filled.

- Read John 6: 5-11. What was Jesus' only request of the people?

If you grew up going to Sunday school, you probably know this story by heart. You've probably retold the story of how Jesus fed the five thousand with just a little boy's five loaves of bread and two tiny fish many times over. But look beyond the miracle, and you see a precious story of Jesus and His people.

Jesus' only request of the people was that they sit down. After He gave thanks for the bread, He distributed to those who were seated as much as they wanted. In the big scheme of this miracle, it seems like such a small, insignificant detail to include in the story. However, this detail holds truths for us still today.

We are a fast-paced society. We eat on the run. Actually, we've gotten good at doing most everything on the run. But notice, Jesus didn't feed these people *on the run*. Jesus wasn't concerned about how fast they got to where they were going. He said, "Have the people sit down." He didn't say, "Ask them if they want to grab a snack to go." He said, "Sit down."

- Is sitting down something that is hard for you? Do you

battle finding a still moment to sit at Jesus feet and feast on His word? Note why.

Notice Jesus only distributed nourishment to those who were seated. He made sure they had as much as they needed. Maybe He had them sit so they'd remember the miracle. Or maybe He had them sit so they could rest in His presence and be satisfied for the rest of the trip.

Later in John 6:28, we find the people asking, "What must we do to do the works God requires?" Mercy, I can hear myself asking that: *What do I need to do? How can I help?* In this mobile society, we put so much weight into "being busy." But Jesus answers, "The work of God is this: to believe in the one he has sent."

What? Jesus mentions nothing to do or to be busy about. Just believe in Jesus. These people wanted signs and wonders. They wanted to be busy doing what God required. They knew the law and the old stories of how their forefathers ate manna in the desert. "As it is written, 'He gave them bread from heaven to eat'" (John 6:31). But Jesus said, "Sit."

Jesus had to explain the bread of the new covenant:

Jesus said to them, "I tell you the truth, it is not Moses who has given you the bread from heaven, but it is my Father who gives you the true bread from heaven. For the bread of God is he who comes down from heaven and gives life to the world."

"Sir," they said, "from now on give us this bread."

Then Jesus declared, "I am the bread of life. He who comes to me will never go hungry, and he who believes in me will never be thirsty. But as I told you, you have seen me and still you do not believe. All that the Father gives me will come to me, and whoever comes to me I will never drive away. (John 6:32-37)

- Who is the bread of God? Describe this passage in your own words.

Manna, or bread of Heaven, fell from the skies while their fore-fathers wandered in the desert. Manna was provided by God in heaven every morning. Do you think they considered that fast food? Probably not! However, Jesus has now come in human form and is still today the Bread of Life. When we come to commune with Him, we will never go hungry. As we sit and partake of His presence, He fills us to overflowing:

Remember how the LORD your God led you all the way in the desert these forty years, to humble you and to test you in order to know what was in your heart, whether or not you would keep his commands. He humbled you, causing you to hunger and then feeding you with manna, which neither you nor your fathers had known, to teach you that man does not live on bread alone but on every word that comes from the mouth of the LORD. (Deut. 8:2, 3)

- What does man live on? How can you feast on the Word of God?

God wants you humble, sitting at the feet of His Son. Feasting in His presence will fill you up. You can't be humble by eating on the go. Likewise, feasting is not eating His Word once a week. Nope! It's time to find God's Word, your Bible, and dust it off. Bring it to the table and feast on God's Word. You'll love it—it's fat free!

Girl, you might have read your Bible through before from Genesis to Revelation, but if you aren't daily devouring the truths of God, you'll never be filled and satisfied. Your house will continually need repair because the blueprints for renovation are contained in His Word.

It is only by sitting down and feasting on the Bread of Life that Jesus can fill you until you've had all you wanted.

Are you lonely? Come and sit.
Are you looking for direction? Come and sit.
Are you hurried, frazzled, or too busy? Come and sit.

Are you questioning and doubting? Come and sit.
Are you down and out? Come and sit.

Jesus calls to us all: "Come to me, all you who are weary and burdened, and I will give you rest. Take my yoke upon you and learn from me, for I am gentle and humble in heart, and you will find rest for your souls" (Matthew 11:28-29).

Linger a bit longer in Jesus' presence. The Bread of Life will take away your burdens, fears, and anxieties if you sit feasting on His word long enough. He wants to satisfy you with His goodness, rest, peace, and grace.

Oh, girl, sit and be filled!

Today's Remodeling Tip:

Carve out a few minutes in your schedule to sit and feast. Bring your Bible to the table. Read Matthew 4:4.

Day Three

The Kitchen Trash

*Y*ou feel yourself full of Jesus' presence as you visit and commune. The Bread of His Presence is definitely satisfying. You are so thankful Jesus has come into your home, and you are becoming more aware of His company, moment by moment.

You offer Him a snack, and He politely accepts. You quickly gather something you have on hand. Placing a big bag of salty tortilla chips, your fabulous home-made salsa, and fresh-baked chocolate chip cookies on the table, you notice Jesus just stares. Looking up He says, "Don't you know that you yourselves are God's temple and that God's Spirit lives in you?" (1 Cor. 3:16).

I don't know if Jesus would have really responded that way. But when you stop and think about it, it's amazing what our modernized culture has done to our eating habits. We have become a fast-paced society that thrives on the fastest, tastiest, and most convenient types of food to prepare. *Oh, shoot— we really don't want to prepare!* We just want to open a bag of chips and down them along with our cola's; we want to zap something in the microwave and be ready to eat in five minutes. Many of our foods are so processed that much of what we eat provides minimal nutrition or wholeness to our body.

Looking at the magazines that grace the check-out counters; one would think we are a society of thin people. However, we are not. Roni DeLuz writes in *21 Pounds in 21 Days*, "Fewer than 5 percent of dieters succeed in keeping the weight they lost off for five years, according to the National Association to Advance Fat Acceptance. A stunning 90 percent of people gain some or all of their weight back, and one-third end up weighing more."[13] Well, that pretty much describes my fight with weight loss. How about you?

The silly thing with us gals is that when someone starts talking about eating healthy, we immediately begin thinking about weight loss. *I know. I'm talking about myself here.* As I began this study, I started changing my eating habits and began consuming mostly natural, healthy foods, and I tried to stay away from caffeine. After a couple of weeks, I weighed and found myself discouraged. As the day went on and I thought about it, I remembered that I had begun eating healthy to glorify God and cleanse out His spiritual house—me. However, that day, I lost my focus and found my mind consumed with weight loss; thus, I ended up discouraged. I had to remind myself that putting healthy foods in my body was for God's glory, not my own.

But let's look more deeply at why Jesus might have just stared at those chips and not dug in like the rest of us would have: "Looking at it one way, you could say, 'Anything goes. Because of God's immense generosity and grace, we don't have to dissect and scrutinize every action to see if it will pass muster.' But the point is not to just get by. We want to live well, but our foremost efforts should be to help others live well" (1 Cor. 10: 23, 24 *Message*).

- In your own words, describe how the above scripture speaks to your heart about what you consume.

To help others live well, we first must live well ourselves by taking care of our bodies—the holy temple of God. It will be a process of scrutinizing every action, of being mindful of what we are doing—especially that hand to mouth action. It will be a process of breaking the old habit of grabbing chips and now reaching for carrot sticks.

"What many of us eat is not very good for us. Our supermarkets and takeout, sit-down, and fast-food restaurants are filled with foods that are high in fat, cholesterol, sodium, artificial flavors and colors, hormones, and preservatives. To make groceries last longer on supermarket shelves, manufacturers strip foods of important nutrients and then 'enrich' them with man-made vitamins and minerals. But the body cannot process man-made ingredients as effectively as the 'real thing'. Because the body doesn't know what to do with any of these synthetic additives, they accumulate inside us as toxins."[14]

Think back to the purity of the garden when God made Adam and Eve. It is no wonder our body cries out; it has no idea how to process or handle all these man-made toxins. These toxins affect our energy levels, moods, and self images.

- Read Daniel 1:1-16. What did the king assign Daniel to eat? What did Daniel ask for instead?

Daniel had resolved not to defile himself with the choice meats, food, and wine. He asks specifically to be served vegetables and water. At the end of those ten days, Daniel and the guys were better nourished and looked healthier. I'm not advocating that you and I live solely off veggies and water. However, I do think we need to be more mindful as to what we are stuffing down the temple of God.

- Write Galatians 6:7-9 in your own words.

Just as we cannot defy the laws of gravity, it would be crazy for us to think we can challenge God's physical laws and win. We will reap what we sow in every aspect of our lives. In Melissa Lancaster's book *Why Are We Sick?*, she tells the story of how her diet had affected her health. She writes, "I came to an understanding that I was reaping what I had sown. I loved my ice cream, white bread products, refined sugar, meat, cheese, chips, and candy. So I thought, 'What's wrong with what I'm eating?' I soon discovered the answer to that question."[15]

Maybe you and I are yet to experience health problems from the fast food and carbonated drinks we ingest daily, but I'm sure the built-up additives taint the windows of our souls. God said, "Look! I have given you every seed-bearing plant throughout the earth and all the fruit trees for your food" (Gen. 1:29 NLT). God *didn't* say, "I have given you a McDonald's, Wendy's®, and Taco Bell® on every corner for your daily intake."

I have to be honest; this is hard for me. As I'm writing this lesson, my daughter is baking chocolate chip cookies. Come on, something is just not right about this. I can hear those cookies calling out my name! *HELP!!!* Seriously though, I've realized it takes planning and preparing ahead of time to be able to eat healthy these days. I don't care to grocery shop, but I'm learning to get over that. I go a couple of times a week now for fresh veggies and fruits. I've learned if I have fresh produce in the house it is easier to make healthy choices. As a bonus, my family eats better too.

Girls, there's no need to become a fanatic. However, it will always be a battle of choices. Remember, I'm not talking about loosing weight, but I am suggesting that you scrutinize what you put into your body, the temple of God: "So whether you eat or drink or whatever you do, do it all for the glory of God" (1 Cor. 10:31). I think I can see why Jesus balked at those chocolate chip cookies.

Today's Remodeling Tip:

Take out the kitchen trash. From the trash remnants, notice the unhealthy choices you've ingested. Determine to eat healthier.

Day Four

It's Not What Goes In

*Y*ou are loving every minute as you linger with Jesus over a healthy snack of carrot sticks and apple slices. Thankfully, you were able to scrounge up something nutritious. In the course of conversation Jesus says, "What you put in your body does not make you unclean. It might make you unhealthy, but not unclean before our Father God. You are so worried about what you put in your body, but yet it is what comes out of your body that makes you unclean."

- Rewrite Matthew 15:10, 11 in your own words.

The Pharisees and teachers were concerned that the disciples were breaking traditions by not washing their hands before they ate. Jesus kindly reminds them that they were breaking the law by enforcing their traditions on others. I guess the old saying is correct—when you point out flaws in somebody else, you have three fingers pointing back at you. *Yikes!* Not only that, but Jesus also tells them they are only full of words and not true worship. Calling them hypocrites, He quotes a scripture from Isaiah 29:13:

> The Lord says:
> "These people come near me with their mouth
> and honor me with their lips,
> but their hearts are far from me.
> Their worship of me
> is made up only of rules taught by men."

Ouch! Remember I said we shouldn't get all fanatical about what we ate? I gave this recommendation because that takes away from *the why* of what we are trying to do—create a better home for God. Yes, He'd like an unpolluted home to live in, but if we are solely focused on what we consume, we are missing the point. Our point should be to make wise decisions that remind us moment by moment that we are the residence of God Almighty.

The key to remembering our true motivation is to tune our hearts into God. Are you confused? If so, that's alright. Peter was as well. Read Matthew 15:15-20.

- When something enters your body, what happens to it? What makes a man unclean? List the things that come out of the heart to make you unclean.

More than anything, Jesus wants clean, pure hearts focused on Him so that what flows out of our mouths will reflect Him. How easily our hearts become unclean with ugly thoughts. If you'll notice, every act listed begins with a thought in the heart: murder, adultery, sexual immorality, theft, false testimony, slander. One doesn't just wake up one day and charge out to murder somebody. No, bitter thoughts began at some point. Then, because these thoughts are not cleansed, the bitterness quickly turns to hatred. Likewise, one doesn't just wake up one morning and have an affair. Instead, it starts with just a little look, an email, a phone call, or a lunch. You get the picture.

Do you remember our lesson "Home Is Where Your Heart Is"? That is exactly why we have to guard our hearts at all times and keep our thoughts turned to God.

- Read Philippians 4:6-8. How do you guard your heart?

Keeping your heart clean will be a challenge. I know. My heart is a difficult place to keep clean, too. But as you fix your thoughts on God, His peace will fill you and guard your heart and mind. You begin guarding your heart by thinking on true, noble, right, pure, lovely, excellent and admirable things (Phil. 4:8).

In a day and age where we are more focused on what we put into our bodies, God wants us to remember it's what comes out that makes us unclean. I'm sure we've all heard the computer term GIGO: garbage in, garbage out. It's even clearer in our spiritual world. If we feed ourselves with vile images, bitterness, and lies, then we can bet that is what will be coming out sooner or later. Once again I find myself thinking, *I'd much rather paint and dress up the exterior than tend to the heart-changing matters on the interior.*

Of course that kind of thinking is totally against God's will and plans for us. As we think about what comes out of our mouths, may we become more mindful of our true heart's focus. I have to wonder if I'm set in my ways like the Pharisees. Do I honor God with my lips, but not my heart?

You see Jesus nodding His head quite approvingly as you begin to understand it's not what goes into you, but what comes out that makes you unclean before God.

Today's Remodeling Tip:

Sit down with a pen and paper. Write down every word out of your mouth so far this day. Have they been pure and pleasing to the Lord?

Day Five

Living Room Idols

After enjoying a healthy snack with Jesus, you ask Him into the living room to get comfortable. You settle in on a comfortable, plush sofa while Jesus takes the wingback chair. You are relaxing in His presence when you suddenly become aware of every little thing in your living room. If only you could do the "flight of the bumble bee."

You are secretly hoping He doesn't flip on the television because there is no telling what will pop up on that screen. You see the magazines on the coffee table and are embarrassed by the cover titles alone. The DVD you rented last night is lying there. The computer is on, and you are praying He won't ask to see what you googled last night. Your eyes notice so many things you'd prefer Jesus not to see.

"I see some idols in here," Jesus says. You're quick to answer, "You'll have to forgive me. I am a huge *American Idol* fan. I confess, I am addicted to the weekly show. Lord, just this season there was a worship leader in the finals."

"You silly girl, I'm not talking about a television show. I'm talking about idols, as in false gods."

You look around confused, "Lord, there are no false gods here. I don't have statues of golden calves or figures of Buddha setting around. What are you referring to?"

Jesus smiles, "You have so much to become aware of, my precious one."

- Read Exodus 34:14. Write out your thoughts.

When God called Moses back up to Mount Sinai to rewrite the stone tablets that Moses had broken, God warned the people not to worship other gods because He is a jealous God. As a matter of fact He said, "Break down their altars, smash their sacred stones and cut down their Asherah poles" (Exodus 34:13). Are you wondering what that command has to do with you today? True, you might not have an Asherah pole (a totem pole of sorts used for worshipping the goddess of fertility) or a stone altar, but you do have objects that take away your focus from God.

Whether you grew up in Sunday school or not, you probably know the first of the Ten Commandments: "You shall have no other gods before me" (Exod. 20:3). But the truth is we all have things that divert our attention away from God. If God is a jealous God, you can bet He wants our undivided attention. He wants to be our number one, our all in all, the only one we look to for help and comfort.

- Write about the things that hold you captive and keep you from focusing on God as number one.

You probably didn't write about carved images standing in the corner of your home or the stone pillars in your back yard. However, there are so many things that capture our focus: people, careers, materialism, or television. Do you read magazines more than you read the word of God? In Kelly Minters book *No Other Gods*, she writes, "Basically, we have edged God out. We have left him with little room in our hearts. Our false gods have taken up our most treasured spaces; we leave God no place to show himself strong on our behalf."[16]

Modern day idols come in many forms. Look around your home. You noticed some of them as you sat down on the couch with Jesus. It's not that every time we watch TV, play the Wii, rent movies, respond to Facebook, read a magazine, or buy a new electronic gadget we are sinning. However, these past times become an idol when we begin to give our sole attention to them. When you have a bad day to whom/to what do you turn? Do you try to forget your troubles by watching the boob-tube or stuffing yourself with a gallon of triple chocolate ice cream?

God wants to be our God. He wants to be our fixer, our comforter, our protector and our companion. He resides within us and is jealous for our attention. He asks, "Is there any God besides me? No, there is no other Rock; I know not one. All who make idols are nothing, and the things they treasure are worthless" (Isa. 44:8, 9).

- Rewrite Matthew 6:19-21 in your own words. Write out how this speaks to you today.

Everything to which we hold on so dearly — our treasures, careers, drugs, friends, entertainment habits, boyfriends, spouses, alcohol, pain killers, food, body image, and self image — will all die in this world. The only thing that will keep us eternally alive is our total focus, love, and devotion to God. He is a jealous God, and it is for our own good that we take His supremacy into consideration. When we are more focused on Him, we are more peaceful, loving, and joyful.

- Read 1 Chronicles 28:9, 10. How are we to serve the Lord? What does the Lord search? Why was Solomon charged to live this way?

As David saw Solomon called to the charge of building the temple, he spoke to his son with words of wisdom, with words from someone who had been there and done that. David knew the only way to build a temple was through wholehearted devotion to the Lord. He was warning his son not to get sidetracked by all the luxuries of the temple, for God would know his heart.

The only way we'll be able to build our spiritual homes on God's solid foundation is if we are wholeheartedly devoted to God. We can't let the world's desires wedge out our true love and source of grace. We have to keep our eyes and hearts tuned into God's music and avoid the trap of today's false gods and images.

I know I will continue to work on eradicating my idols until the day I see Jesus face to face. There are so many things that easily steal my attention and divert my focus away from God. As we've covered so many rooms this week, you might be feeling a little overwhelmed. That overwhelming feeling should not overtake you; rather, let that feeling make you more aware that you house the God of gods.

Jesus leans forward from His chair and whispers, "Girl, you're getting it now."

Dear Heavenly Father, I have enjoyed sitting with you at the table this week. You have opened my eyes to things that draw my attention away from you, as well as things that pollute my body. Help me be more intentional in the way I live for you. Amen.

Today's Remodeling Tip:

Sit down in your living room. Look around and notice the things that excessively draw your attention away from God. Can you do without them or at least limit your time with them?

Week Six
Standing Firm and on Guard

*I*t didn't take long before our family was settled into the dream home my dad built, and we were enjoying everything about it. Our first Christmas was memorable. There was a fire going almost every evening in the large two-way fireplace.

As the next summer rolled around, my brother, sister, and I were playing outside one evening when our eyes were drawn to the sky where a gathering of flying birds had begun circling the neighborhood houses. As we watched even closer, we began to notice the flying creatures were honing in on our home. Looking like something out of the thriller movie *Birds*, we called our parents outside to witness this swarm of black birds.

The flock grew bigger, and they began circling up in a tighter formation. We soon noticed them dipping into our chimney. One or two would drop abruptly into the chimney every few minutes, and then the whole flock spiraled suddenly into the chimney as if they were being sucked down a drain.

Amazed, we ran inside to hear the faint chirps of these Chimney Sweeps settling inside our chimney as they began to roost. Unfortunately, we had not yet cleared the fireplace of last year's Christmas memories. You can just imagine the smell of soot as the ashes now covered everything in the house: stinky, dusty, gross.

As we finish our study, my prayer for you is that you will thoroughly sweep your house clean and stay on guard from here forward. When the study is complete and the final page is turned, don't let the words of God fall silent. Keep them tucked away in your heart to help guard the house of your soul, the house of your God.

Day One

The Hall Closet

*I*t is hard for me to believe we are at our last week together. I am being remodeled and restored daily. Some days I balk. Some days I delight in the change. But overall, I am enjoying the new sense that I am truly Jesus' home. I hope you are, too.

At the moment, are you enjoying your visit with Jesus? He has given you so much to consider and work towards. You haven't felt condemned since He reminded you He left his hammer at the cross. You are so thankful because He has brought so much into the light. You are relaxing and finding refreshment in His presence when Jesus asks to peer inside your hall closet. *WAIT, NOT THE HALL CLOSET,* you scream on the inside. *Oops! Did Jesus hear that?* You're praying He doesn't actually open that hall door. He'll be in for a surprise if He does. Seriously, the whole mess will tumble out upon Him.

As you near the hall closet, Jesus mentions he smells some kind of a stench. You think that comment seems rather rude. You've spent the day together, and He's examined your foundation, water, power, dining and living room, not to mention the kitchen trash. And now He wants to see a hall closet. Jesus, knowing your thoughts, says, "I can't fully live in a house with this odor. The smell is stifling."

When Jesus utters those words, you know exactly what He's talking about. "In that closet you have one or two little personal things you don't want anybody to know about. Certainly, you don't want Christ to see them. They were dead and rotting things leftover from the old life—not wicked, but not right and good to have in a Christian life. You are afraid to admit they were there."[17]

- Write out James 3:13-16. What might you be hiding in your hall closet?

If we harbor bitterness, envy, and selfish ambition in the closets of our hearts, it is unspiritual. Bitterness will eventually eat you alive. Those wrongful acts that have been committed against you are just that—wrong. However, to claim the full life Jesus came to give, you have to come to the realization that you can't hide or hang on to those old wounds and feelings. The day has come when you must let them go. Today is the perfect day. Jesus is waiting to take them and their stench away.

It is for our own good that Jesus wants to take away those selfish desires. Are you holding and hiding feelings of resentment over lost opportunities and dreams of your past? Are you hiding under the excuse of being wronged or scammed? Do you think you have every right to feel the things you feel?

As someone who harbored feelings of anger for years, I can personally tell you those emotions will zap every once of life out of you. When the feelings become enraged, they can harm you physically, mentally, and spiritually. It's a work in progress to let them go, but it is so worth it.

Have you ever cleaned out your hall closet? If it's as messy as mine, it is an all day process. Then to make matters more difficult, the clutter gets worse as you begin cleaning. Finally, after some time, it begins to take shape, look clean, and smell refreshed. The same is true of our spiritual selves.

- Look up the following scriptures and list what we should **not** harbor in our hall closets.
    Job 36:13
    Proverbs 26:24
    Jeremiah 4:14
    Ezekiel 35:4-6

So maybe your hostility didn't end in blood shed, but has it brought you to the place of avoiding people? Do you hold grudges while vindictive thoughts race through your mind? Have the resentments of yesterday, or even of today, caused you to puff yourself up with pride to prove yourself? Does the stench in your closet lead you to lie in hopes of covering up your real self? Or, do you have wicked thoughts more often than you'd care to admit?

Girls, it's time to gut out this closet, give it a nice new coat of paint, and let Jesus make it new again. It's no wonder Jesus can't reside where the stink is. I don't even want to reside with myself when I'm holding on to the decay of my past. It's worse than the smell of old ash and soot; it is the smell of death.

Growing up, I always tried to maintain my "good girl, good Christian" image. In doing so, there were all kinds of skeletons and masks hanging in my closet. Years ago, when a scam artist took my husband and me for everything, the FBI came knocking on our door. Because I was so used to wearing a mask, I certainly didn't want my friends to know what we were going through. There was so much anger, bitterness, and resentment to cram in my hall closet that the door would no longer shut. As I tried to shove the door closed one day, I broke down. Calling a friend for help she told me, "If you let the secrets go, they will have no power over you. You won't need to hide them any longer."

Oh girl, there is power in confession and cleaning! Once I opened the closet and threw out the skeletons, I could close the door again. The foul odor was gone, and I felt free. There is freedom in confessing those old habits, hang ups, and hurts. Fling open your hall closet door today, and let Jesus free you from your past and your hurts. Girl, you will love the guilt-free feeling.

Today's Remodeling Tip:

Clean out your hall closet. Decide what needs to be thrown out or given to Goodwill. During the process, think about what needs to be thrown out of your spiritual life. Confess it and feel free.

Day Two

Sweeping Out the House

*Y*ou're beginning to feel more peace now that the hall closet is cleaned out; however, there is still a mess. All those hidden things you drug out of the closet are now cluttering up your home. "Jesus, now what am I suppose to do," you ask with frustration. He gathers the broom and dust pan and says, "You sweep until they are gone."

You begin sweeping with a back and forth motion, thinking this is absolutely doing no good. You hear Jesus whisper, "So clean house! Make a clean sweep of malice and pretense, envy and hurtful talk. You've had a taste of God. Now, like infants at the breast, drink deep of God's pure kindness" (1 Pet. 2:1-3 *Message*).

"Um, Jesus, I don't mean to be rude, but how is this going to help? How is sweeping going to free my mind from these awful thoughts and habits?"

"Actually this won't help unless you follow a simple equation. For every thing you sweep out—anger, greed, lust, shame—you must replace it with something else." Walking back towards the kitchen table, Jesus says over his shoulder, "Grab your Bible and let's read a story."

- Read Luke 11:24-26. What is the simple equation for keeping the house swept clean?

Let's look *at The Message* version of this passage:

When a corrupting spirit is expelled from someone, it drifts along through the desert looking for an oasis, some unsuspecting soul it can bedevil. When it doesn't find anyone, it says, "I'll go back to my old haunt." On return, it finds the person swept and dusted, but vacant. It then runs out and rounds up seven other spirits dirtier than itself and they all move in, whooping it up. That person ends up far worse than if he'd never gotten cleaned up in the first place.

As you sweep out those dirty thoughts, sins, and unclean behaviors, you will begin to feel free. Remember the feeling you had yesterday after you cleaned out your hall closet? The freedom that came from confessing and letting go of those old, stinky sins and attitudes felt good, just as it should. If you are to put yourself into the story above, the corrupting spirit has now left your home. He is now roaming the neighborhood, looking for some other unsuspecting soul to devour. That will be too much work for the little devil, so he'll come back and look in on your house. He will be thrilled. Your house is swept and clean, yet void of any presence. Mainly, void of God's presence. In other words, the house is vacant. Seeing the emptiness, the evil spirit goes and finds his other stinky pals to move in, and the stench returns.

The simple fact is you cannot sweep yourself empty. Remember this equation: To turn away from something, you must turn to something. Better yet, turn to Someone!

- Check some of these things that need to be swept out of your house:
  - _____gossip
  - _____irritations
  - _____laziness
  - _____excessive spending
  - _____impatience
  - _____need for control
  - _____hatred

_____excessive drinking
_____prayerlessness
_____lying
_____anger
_____guilt

I'm sure each of us could come up with many things that need to be swept out of our homes. But unless we are replacing those things with Someone, they are surely to come back and haunt us. Think about it. You've probably already experienced this in your own life in some form.

You decide to break a bad habit; let's say you decide to stop smoking. You gear yourself up and pick your day to quit. You do well for a couple of days, maybe even weeks or months, but then the craving becomes so bad that you give in. Notice here, did you replace that old habit with anything new? No. Now that you've given in to your own desire again, you want more than you had before, and the desire seems unquenchable. The problem is you never replaced the old habit with Someone. A void was left. Therefore, the devil and his pals snuck back in.

- Read Romans 15:13 and Philippians 1:9-11. What are you to be filled with to avoid the emptiness?

It sounds so easy; of course we would want the God of hope to fill us with joy, knowledge, insight, discernment, and peace as we trust in Him while we cleanse ourselves. However, it takes diligence to make that happen. 1 Peter 1:13, 14 says, "Therefore, prepare your minds for action; be self-controlled; set your hope fully on the grace to be given you when Jesus Christ is revealed. As obedient children, do not conform to the evil desires you had when you lived in ignorance."

We have to be prepared for action and full of self-control. There comes a time when we can no longer conform to our desires and live in ignorance. It is time to sweep our lives clean.

As we end our study together, are you becoming aware of the things that need to be swept out of your life? Is Jesus making known the attitudes and habits that are polluting your spiritual house? Are you beginning to feel overwhelmed or guilty because you haven't succeeded yet?

Jesus, sensing your thoughts says, "I don't want you to feel overwhelmed. Cleaning your spiritual house is a process you will work on every day of your life. Let's read another story together."

- Read John 8:1-11. What are Jesus words to this woman?

You might have drug out enough dust, grit, grime and clutter from the hall closet of your soul that Jesus can actually bend down and write in the mess. Nevertheless, He loves you, just as He loved this adulterous woman. He doesn't criticize or condemn you. He forgives, but He does ask that you go and sin no more.

A life renewed and swept clean from the inside out is a life focused on Christ. Communing with Him daily and feasting on His word is how we will keep the raging devil away:

So let God work his will in you. Yell a loud no to the Devil and watch him scamper. Say a quiet yes to God and he'll be there in no time. Quit dabbling in sin. Purify your inner life. Quit playing the field. Hit bottom, and cry your eyes out. The fun and games are over. Get serious, really serious. Get down on your knees before the Master; it's the only way you'll get on your feet. (James 4:7-10 Message)

That, my friend, is how you can maintain a clean closet and a home that is swept and stench free. As you fill yourself with God's way of life from His word, He creates new habits and desires within you. He reproduces His character in you, His residence.

Today's Remodeling Tip:
Vacuum your house. Think about how you can replace your old habits. Examples: Instead of gossiping, speak His praises. Replace excessive drinking with big gulps of Living Water.

Day Three

A Place of Prayer

*L*ingering in Jesus' presence at your table, you find yourself not wanting Him to leave. You have felt such contentment and joy while communing with Him. As He shares stories from Scripture, it's as if all the troubles and cares you carry are lifted. It's just you and Him lost in the moment of conversation when He says, "It's nearing my time to move on and knock at your neighbor's door. Do you have any last questions about your spiritual house?"

Wanting to cry, you squeak out, "Jesus, you can't leave. This old house is not totally swept clean and put together yet. Can you stay longer? Pleeeeeeeease!"

Consider Hebrews 13: 5, 6: "God has said, 'Never will I leave you; never will I forsake you.' So we say with confidence, 'The Lord is my helper; I will not be afraid. What can man do to me?'"

- Write the above scripture replacing *you* with your own name.

Thankfully, Jesus never leaves. He dwells within you. You might turn your back on Him or forget He is there, but He never leaves. You might feel like you've lost Him, but He hasn't moved.

- Read Luke 15:8-10. What has the woman lost? How would you feel if you lost a whole day's pay? What does God do?

133

Have you ever misplaced or lost a large sum of money? Panic, urgency, and passion to find the currency take over. You can't sleep or think of anything else. You search and you search. The loss consumes your thoughts. If you haven't lost money, consider losing a child. The child is there with you in the store. You turn around, and she is gone. Heart-throbbing urgency and fear take over.

I had a dream last night that I lost a book of lessons that the Lord had given me. I was in a panic. I searched from room to room. I looked behind couches and under furniture. My soul would not rest until I found those lessons. I woke myself up from the dream in a panic. Actually, it was more of a nightmare!

If you are feeling like you've lost Jesus, stir up some urgency and passion to search for Him. The angels of God will be rejoicing and cheering you on as you repent and begin to search for Him. When you seek Him with your whole heart and have such a passion to know Him, you'll find Him. He'll show up and His words will change your life. And girl, you don't have to search far and long to find him.

- Read Psalm 119:9-16. Paraphrase this passage in your own words. Where will He be found?

How can you keep your way pure? How can you continually be in the presence of Jesus? Simple, you stay in His Word. Live according to His Word and don't neglect His Word. Keep God's Word hidden within your heart. Jesus did the same when He walked here upon earth. He knew the Scriptures and lived by their every word. Recall the story when Jesus was just a boy and strayed from his parents because He had to be in the temple courts sitting with the teachers, listening and asking questions (Luke 2:43-46).

Jesus knew God's Word. He knew the Scriptures that had been handed down on the scrolls from generation after generation. God's Word is what kept Him holy and pure as He was tempted in the desert by Satan. Those precious words were hidden inside Jesus' heart, and He was able to stand strong against the evil one.

Jesus knew how important it was to make time for the Father and His Word. If the sinless One needs time with His Father, how much more time should we need with God and His Word. When Jesus was trapped, spat upon, neglected, betrayed, questioned, frustrated, and even tired, He withdrew from the craziness to be with God. Even when He was serving and healing, He made time to be with His Father.

- Write out Luke 5:16.

As often as possible, Jesus "withdrew to lonely places to pray." We can learn a lot from that one sentence. No matter what Jesus was going through, He made time to be with the Father to gain strength and understanding. Even when He was busy fulfilling His call to ministry and was healing many, He found time to take a break in His schedule and withdraw to an out-of-the-way place for prayer. The place was free of distractions and out of the way of others, just like Moses' tent of meeting. He purposefully planned to spend time communing with the Father for wisdom and refreshment.

- Do you have such a place to withdraw to for prayer and reading God's word? Despite your schedule, do you make time to be with the Father?

If not, make today the day you find a special spot free of distractions where you can commune with the Father. Prayer means communicating. It takes two—one to listen and one to hear. When you pray, God hears your prayers just as He has promised. To hear from God and understand what He has to say, you need time in His Word. His Word is "living and active" (Hebrews 4:12, 13). It is "useful for teaching, rebuking, correcting and training in righteousness, so that the man of God may be thoroughly equipped for every good work" (2 Timothy 3:16, 17).

It is through spending time in prayer and study that we are made aware of how to build and fix-up our spiritual homes. God gives us a word, just when we need it. He gave Jesus the stamina and strength when He needed it, but Jesus first went to the Father.

Where will your place of prayer be? Will it be a favorite wing-back chair, a cozy spot on the couch, or your kitchen table? Decide today where your communication spot with the Lord will be and begin working it into your schedule. Jesus will never leave you, but your responsibility is to go to Him and visit regularly. He is there waiting at your favorite spot. He has much to tell you. Will you meet him there?

Today's Remodeling Tip:

Now that you've determined your place of prayer, get out your calendar and plan to meet the Lord in your communication spot daily. Remember to bring your Bible and prepare your heart to hear from Him.

Day Four

The Sweet Aroma

$\mathcal{Y}$ou're looking deep into Jesus' eyes as if to beg Him not to leave your presence when He leans forward, "Dear One, committing to and making time to spend with Me is not for my benefit. Yes, I will certainly enjoy our every moment together, and I will be waiting for you to join Me daily. However, there are incredible benefits to you and your spiritual house to be gained through your time with me. I must be going, but remember I'm just a conversation away."

When Solomon finished building the temple, he dedicated and consecrated it before the Lord. The Lord then spoke to Solomon:

> *I have heard your prayer and have chosen this place for myself as a temple for sacrifices. When I shut up the heavens so that there is no rain, or command locusts to devour the land or send a plague among my people, if my people, who are called by my name, will humble themselves and pray and seek my face and turn from their wicked ways, then will I hear from heaven and will forgive their sin and will heal their land. Now my eyes will be open and my ears attentive to the prayers offered in this place. I have chosen and consecrated this temple so that my Name may be there forever. My eyes and my heart will always be there. (2 Chron. 7:12-16)*

- When the people were at their lowest, what did God ask them to do?

When there was no rain, no food, and total chaos, God simply asked them to humble themselves and pray. I'm sure they were wondering where their answers were and what good prayer would do. But through their prayers, God forgave the sin and healed their land. God promises the same for your spiritual house. If you will call upon Him, He will heal you of your bad habits and forgive your sin. God has chosen to live in you forever. His eyes and heart will always be with you.

- Write out Psalm 5:3.

Your responsibility is to lay your requests before the Lord, day in and day out, whether or not the circumstances make sense. You wait, but not while moaning and groaning. You wait in expectation of how God will answer that prayer. You wait with your eyes open to see Him move and work miracles. You wait in eager expectation that He has heard you and will provide the best answer for you.

Honestly, that kind of waiting is hard. I feel like I know the best answers for me. I figure out the way things should be, and then I wait and watch for the way I think God should answer. I have to remind myself that while God listens to my prayers, He already sees the glorious end; I can't. God answers with heaven in mind, while I want answers this moment. The wait is tough. Often, frustration sets in and sometimes my passion for prayer is lost. Can you relate?

But God says never give up. Never quit praying. Never stop seeking Him.

- Write in your own words the prayer of David in Psalm 141:1, 2.

Oh my, I can so relate to David. I feel like I'm continually asking God to hear me and answer quickly. Looking back over the years, if God would have answered upon my first request, I would have missed out on learning so much from Him. Our Father truly does know best. Not only that, but He also appreciates our prayers and the fragrant aroma that accompanies them. Our prayers are the sweet aroma and praise of His home.

Home fragrance is big today. You can buy any type of aroma in candle, incense, or a wall plug-in. I love walking into a home that has a fresh fragrance. God wants our spiritual homes full of satisfying scents as it is a reminder of what we have waiting at the throne in heaven.

- Read Revelation 5:8. What are the golden bowls in heaven full of?

Imagine our prayers filling the golden bowls in heaven. A sweet aroma fills the heavens, and God takes pleasure in the odor. When our prayers fill heaven with beautiful scents, they also fill our spiritual homes. You can be knee deep in renovation with the smell of sawdust and power tools everywhere, but the sweet fragrance of your prayers will billow up from it all and erase the stench.

A friend entered my home one day. After she'd been here a minute she sighed, "Peace. There is so much peace in this home. Can I just sit and enjoy the peace I am feeling?" I have to admit the statement took me by surprise. She was most sincere and asked to be left alone in my living room for a moment. I left, and she soaked up the peace she was feeling. Are you longing for that sense of peace?

There is another benefit to committing time and prayer to the Lord. Peace, girl! You will feel so much peace. You won't be able to help it; Jesus is peace.

- Read the following scriptures. What does the Lord provide?
    Psalm 29:11
    Psalm 85:8
    1 Thessalonians 5:23

When you commune with the Lord, He fills you with peace. He gives you strength for your day's troubles and gifts you with a peace that surpasses all understanding. His sweet peaceful aroma fills your heart. He will help you stay away from where you have come from. So, you might still feel like a fixer-upper, but He won't turn His back on you. The Master Renovator calls from within, telling you to rest in His peace and continue your day-by-day process of remodeling. Your little shanty might one day be a palace and along the journey, you'll not become discouraged, disheartened, or disenchanted because you have the peace of God dwelling within you.

It will continue to be a process of renovation all the days of your life. Hallelujah, you have the Lord of peace within as you make this journey. He will sustain you, through your prayers, with His peace.

Ah, the sweet aroma. Can you smell it?

Today's Remodeling Tip:

Light a fragrant candle. Sit and enjoy the pleasant aroma while thanking God for the peace He provides while the renovation is taking place.

Day Five

Set the Alarm

*I*t's our last day together. Jesus has made it apparent that it is time for Him to move on, and you might be feeling a little lonely and discouraged. Standing with Jesus at the front door, He reminds you that He loves you and asks you to set the alarm when He leaves. You send Him off with a hug, "I love you too, Lord, but why set the alarm?"

Renovating your house is hazardous work. It's no wonder you need a hard hat. Christ has called you to remodel so that you can be more like Him, yet you need to stay alert and on guard. You've become aware over the last six weeks that this is a large job He has called you to. However, Jesus knows that once you set the alarm, you can continue on with the process, knowing warning sounds will go off if traps appear to trip you up.

In 1995, I had children ranging in age from two to five. It was the worse spring ever. The kids were continually sick. Moms, you know how it goes. One gets sick, and he/she gets well just in time for another kid to get sick, etc. It was horrible. After six weeks of being cooped up in the house, I couldn't stand it. I awoke one morning to a fresh spring day and decided I would clean the house from top to bottom. Those germs were going to die!

I cleaned all day and felt a sense of freshness coming back to the house. The breeze was cool and refreshing that day, so I flung open the front door so the kids could enjoy it. Shortly thereafter, it started to rain. The kids were enjoying sitting in the door way and watching it rain, so I went about my business. All of the sudden I heard squealing. I ran to the door only to find a huge, hairy stray dog in our house, wet, dirty, and shaking his filth all over my freshly cleaned house. *Urgh!*

- Read and summarize 1 Peter 5:8, 9 in your own words.

As restoration continues, you need to be self-controlled and alert. The devil and his evil friends are looking for a way to blow up and destroy your newly remodeled home. He comes in many ways—even as a wet, shaggy, stray dog. He's not just looking; he is prowling around, looking to pounce and devour everything you've worked so hard for. He'll huff, and he'll puff, and he will try to blow your house down! You've got to keep your eyes open and your alarm set so you are more aware than ever when he is drawing in close. Stand strong, resist him and his temptations, and then you will succeed.

- Read James 4:6-8. What does this verse say to your heart?

Submitting ourselves to God by obeying Him helps us stand strong against the evil one. After we resist the evil one and his snares a few times, he'll give up and move on. However, now that we have knowledge, it will be easy for us to say, "Oh, I know that!" Knowing Scripture and being diligent to stand upon what it says are two different things. That is why, in the verse above, God says He opposes the proud. He's not looking for a know-it-all. He's looking for the humble, one that is obedient and moldable. He wants one who will stand firm:

These words I speak to you are not incidental additions to your life, homeowner improvements to your standard of living. They are foundational words, words to build a life on. If you work these words into your life, you are like a smart carpenter who built his house on solid rock. Rain poured down, the river flooded, a tornado hit—but nothing moved that house. It was fixed to the rock. But if you just use my words in Bible studies and don't work them into your life, you are like a stupid carpenter who built his house on the sandy beach. When a storm rolled in and the waves came up, it collapsed like a house of cards. (Matt. 7:24-27 Message)

- Explain how you have used God's Word and this Bible study to remodel your life these past six weeks.

My prayer is that your eyes have been opened and your heart has accepted the fact that you are God's house. What you have spent time learning is not a waste of time; it is a way of life, waiting for you to embrace it for all your days to come. It won't be easy. You've already discovered that this is hard work; you have counted the cost for change in an earlier lesson. However, the peace that will fill your spiritual house as you strive to build and remodel based on biblical principals is priceless. These principals will never go out of style—they are truth, and they are ageless.

Some days I still feel like a fixer-upper; however, change has taken place. Remodeling has begun. During our time together, I have began quoting our memory scriptures, drinking more water while thinking about Christ's living water, and eating more fruits and vege-tables as I remind myself that Christ is the Bread of Life. Change hasn't only been outward. Renovation has begun on the inside, too. I've swept away negative thoughts and feelings (resentment, shame, and guilt) and replaced them with positive praise and prayer. I've gone to my private place of prayer and communed with my Father often. These changes might not seem like much to you, but they have been monumental to me—just as your changes are to you.

During our six-weeks together, we have seen Moses answer God's call to build a tabernacle as God wanted to dwell with his people. We also witnessed Moses methodically carrying out every detail to build that tabernacle. Through these weeks, God has spoken to our souls about how He wants to dwell within us. He wants continual fellowship and longs to meet us for conversation in our place of prayer. Hallelujah, God meant what He said: "I want to dwell with my people" (Exod. 29:46).

Through this study, have you become more mindful that resto-ration and remodeling is a process? In our opening week, you saw that the temple was torn down and rebuilt many times. Can you see how that relates to your own life? Look back through your journal, and you will become aware of how much you've already accomplished. Read over the lists you've made and continue to work on them. Check items off when they are accomplished or conquered. During the process, set your alarm.

And remember, Jesus is here. Pick up His Word often to continue your remodeling job. You are becoming a beautiful home in which God loves to dwell. I hope you can feel His peace beaming out the windows of your soul.

Stay on guard, girl! You've got a good thing going. You might have started as a fixer-upper, but you're now fixed-up because you are fixed on God. I'm so proud of you!

Today's Remodeling Tip . . .

Read Mark 13:32-37. Reflect on why the remodeling needs to be done now.

Resources for Remodeling

Week One: Tents, Tabernacles, and Temples—Oh, My

1 Eric Sandras, PhD., Plastic Jesus, Exposing the Hollowness of Comfortable Christianity (Colorado Springs: NavPress, 2006), 112.

2 Sandras, PhD., 114.

3 Alec Garrard, The Splendor of the Temple (Grand Rapids: Kregel, 2000), 12.

4 Rob Lacey, The Word on the Street (Grand Rapids: Zondervan, 2004), 268.

Week Two: A Guest or a Resident

5 W. H. Monk (music), Henry F. Lyte (lyrics), "Abide with Me."

Week Three: Change Is Here

6 Roy B. Zuck, The Speaker's Quote Book (Grand Rapids: Kregel, 1997), 167.

7 Bible History Online, "The Healing at the Pool of Bethesda," http://www.bible-history.com/sketches/ancient/pool-bethesda.html.

8 Meshel/Welch/Bloodworth, "It's a Sunshine Day," The Best of the Brady Bunch (Sony/ATV Music).

9 A.J. Russell, God Calling (Uhrichsville: Barbour, 1953), 77.

Week Four: The Carpenter
10 Rick Warren, The Purpose Driven Life (Grand Rapids: Zondervan, 2002), 180.
11 Max Lucado, Come Thirsty (Nashville: W Publishing, 2004), 11, 12.

Week Five: Put Your House in Order
12 "The Bread of the Presence", His Firedancer's Weblog, http://hisfiredancer.wordpress.com/2008/03/07/the-bread-of-the-presence.
13 Roni DeLuz, RN, ND, 21 Pounds in 21 Days – The Martha's Vineyard Diet Detox (New York: Harper Collins, 2007), 24.
14 Roni DeLuz, RN, ND, 30-31.
15 Melissa Lancaster, Why Are We Sick? (BookSurge.com, 2008), 12.
16 Kelly Minter, No Other Gods – Confronting Our Modern Day Idols (Colorado Springs: David C. Cook, 2008), 19.

Week Six: Standing Firm and on Guard
17 Robert Boyd Munger, My Heart—Christ's Home (Downers Grove: InterVarsity Press, 1986), 17.

About the Author

*S*truggling to know more about this person God created her to be, Alene Snodgrass became aware of the self-doubt and insecurities that were tearing down her spiritual house and darkening the windows of her soul. She became a pro at hiding her feelings of inadequacy and applying coats of paint to cover up her true self.

A few years ago, Alene was asked to speak at a conference. Arriving at the conference, she checked the speaker line up and saw there were incredible speakers before her—you know, the ones with testimonies that leave you sitting on the edge of your seat. As she took the stage, she questioned what she was doing. The words plaguing her mind were, *I'm so ordinary; I don't even have a testimony! I'll never measure up.* She realized then that she had quite a bit of fixing-up and remodeling to do in her spiritual house.

By sheer grace and acts of God, Alene has spoken all over the country. Her first Bible study, *Dirty Laundry Secrets ~ a Journey to Meet the Launderer*, has created drastic changes in many women. She has also been published in numerous books and written weekly devotionals for years.

To find out more about Alene or her ministry, contact her online at www.alenesnodgrass.com. She would love to speak at your next event.

LaVergne, TN USA
09 January 2010
169447LV00004B/10/P